Unlearning Meditation

Unlearning
Meditation

*What to Do When
the Instructions Get in the Way*

Jason Siff

Shambhala
Boston & London
2010

SHAMBHALA PUBLICATIONS, INC.
Horticultural Hall
300 Massachusetts Avenue
Boston, Massachusetts 02115
www.shambhala.com

9 8 7 6 5 4 3 2 1

First Edition
Printed in the United States of America

∞ This edition is printed on acid-free paper that meets the American
National Standards Institute z39.48 Standard.
♻ This book was printed on 30% postconsumer recycled paper. For
more information please visit www.shambhala.com.

Distributed in the United States by Random House, Inc.,
and in Canada by Random House of Canada Ltd

Designed by Daniel Urban-Brown

Library of Congress Cataloging-in-Publication Data

Siff, Jason.
Unlearning meditation: what to do when the instructions get
in the way / Jason Siff.—1st ed.
    p.   cm.
Includes index.   ·
ISBN 978-1-59030-752-6 (pbk.: alk. paper)
1. Meditation—Buddhism. I. Title.
BQ5612.S54 2010
294.3'4435—DC22
                              2010004658

To Jeremy Tarcher

Contents

INTRODUCTION

Moving Beyond Meditator's Guilt

When I am invited to teach a new group of meditators, I like to know how each person meditates and, generally, what kinds of experiences they have. So I begin by asking them to say a little something about their meditation practice. The first thing almost everyone says is, "I don't meditate every day." This is said with a hint of shame.

I might then reply with this compassionate suggestion, "You can meditate when you feel like meditating."

But then someone will usually say, "But aren't we supposed to meditate every day?" And then they sometimes ask me, "Don't you meditate every morning?"

This is meditator's guilt. It goes deep into the fabric of how we learn to meditate. Because when we learn how to meditate, we try to do the instructions perfectly, setting high standards for ourselves. We consequently experience periods of failure and inadequacy, along with the occasional moments of success, but it all adds up to guilt at not meditating often enough, not doing it well enough, not being the ideal meditator. And then we may also push ourselves too hard, sit with too much pain for too long, become intolerant of being caught up in our thoughts and feelings, and feel ashamed by the strength and tenacity of undesirable emotions.

I've met quite a few people in the past two decades who, at one time or another, have either given up on meditation out of frustration or kept doing a meditation practice that is giving them more grief than peace. It doesn't have to be this way. There are alternatives. The method I teach, called Recollective Awareness Meditation, is one of them.

Just as we go through a period of learning how to meditate, we can also go through a period of *un*learning meditation. This book will provide guidance on how to engage that process and in doing so will present the meditation experiences of people going through it. By reading other people's experiences, you may find you are not alone in this—that others have been through a period of unlearning the unwanted habits of their meditation practice and have arrived at a new commitment to meditation, along with a greater interest in, and appreciation of, their inner worlds.

I encounter many people who, once they hear that I am a meditation teacher, tell me that they can't meditate because they think too much. Some of them are professors, scientists, and psychologists, who use their thinking in their work and have developed as human beings through using their minds. Because they have gotten a picture of meditation as requiring a quiet, thought-free mind, they feel they can't do it. That is a real loss, a true shame. Recollective Awareness is an approach to meditation that not only doesn't prohibit thinking, but teaches a way of looking into your thoughts so that you can learn things about the thinking process itself. By taking this approach, paradoxically, many people find that their thinking minds actually quiet down, and they find themselves more able to focus on the physical and emotional sides of their experiences.

The effects of unlearning meditation can be many and varied. A wide range of emotions can arise. What has been hidden from awareness can be revealed. And people open up to a wide range of calm, tranquil states of mind. This can be a powerful meditation practice. But it is not for everyone; no single meditation practice is. It meets the needs of those experienced meditators who are seeking a gentle, open, and insightful form of meditation, as well as those who are new to meditation and are looking for a simple and effective way to begin a meditation practice.

Unlearning Meditation is *not* a book that rejects traditional meditation practices. You are not asked to drop your existing meditation practice for good and take up an altogether new form of meditation. Instead, this book provides observations and insights into how people meditate, what they experience, and what would be useful and skillful ways of being with what comes up in meditation sittings for most people. In my two decades of teaching meditation, there have been many instances of people who have unlearned specific meditation practices, only to return later to those practices with greater flexibility and interest, move on to another practice, or even develop their own way of meditating.

This approach to meditation comes directly out of my practice and study of the Dharma. It may appear to be more psychologically oriented than many other approaches, since it is a meditation practice for becoming aware of your thoughts and feelings; understanding your views, ideals, and beliefs; and seeing into how your mind functions both skillfully and otherwise. The kinship between psychotherapy and meditation is there, naturally, but the agendas are often different, and their direction (or trajectory) is different also. The value of Recollective Awareness, and I would say of Buddhist meditation practices in general, is to become aware of the dependently arisen nature of all mental phenomena and, through that way of knowing one's experience, to become wiser, gentler, and more peaceful.

The Buddhist concept of dependent arising, or dependent origination, is a way of looking at things that lies at the heart of meditation practice. The basic principle of dependent origination is, simply stated, that certain states, or conditions, naturally and inevitably lead to others: "When one thing is, so is another; when one thing arises, so does another." Our inner worlds are complex and varied, and each experience is composed of interrelated elements. Dependent arising is fundamentally a way of knowing how our experiences are put together and how they are kept alive.

With this method, we are first trying to get to know our mind by being gentle and permissive rather than starting out being disciplinarians. Meditation does not have to be an exercise to do, a chore to get through, or a thing to accomplish. It is through gentleness and kindness to ourselves in meditation that we can learn how to become genuinely interested in how our mind operates: we can make astute observations, pursue avenues of exploration, test out hypotheses. When you are interested in the dependently arisen inner world of your meditation sittings, meditator's guilt has no hold or sway over you. Your reasons for meditating are your own.

PART ONE

Unlearning
Meditation

The Basic Practice

1

Being Realistic about Meditation

Meditation is about a tension between allowing *your mind as it is* and *the meditation instructions you use.* The story of meditation, regardless of the tradition, is about the way our wandering mind and the meditation instructions work together, fight, or try to have nothing to do with each other. Most people think there should be perfect harmony between your mind and the meditation instruction you're following—this is *meditation, after all!* That's a romantic idea of meditation.

What we are concerned with here are realistic experiences of meditation, ones that feature conflicts, doubts, and desires as well as peaceful states, profound insights, and deep internal changes. Each person's meditation experience is a story with many dimensions to it—it is never an account of following an instruction perfectly and then someday achieving the promise of that practice. It just doesn't happen to real people that way. At least not to anyone I know.

The kinds of meditation stories I'm most familiar with are about unlearning meditation. While learning meditation involves adhering to particular instructions, unlearning meditation is a way of meditating that acknowledges *your mind as it is* in meditation and explores the tension that exists between that and the instructions. It is a way both to unlearn an existing meditation practice and to begin a new one. The descriptions of meditation sittings in this book come from students who have embarked on a meditation practice that begins with allowing *your mind as it is* in meditation.

I will begin with my own story.

When I started meditating at age fourteen, I was first given the instruction to focus on a mantra, as was the common practice back then. I would sit for twenty to thirty minutes trying to stay with the single-syllable sound, repeating it over or lengthening the sound, attempting to fill all of my time in meditation with it, reminding myself to keep it alive whenever my mind wandered. I didn't stick with that practice for more than a few weeks, as it didn't seem to do anything. During that period of my life, I would also take time out during the day to lie on my back on a couch or sit in an armchair with my eyes closed. At those times I would let my mind wander and allow myself to go to sleep if I was so inclined. Often I just thought about things, usually about what I was reading, mostly Eastern religion and existentialism. But occasionally, I would flow into a state where I watched parades of inner images, and with that came a certain lightness and joy. I wouldn't have called it meditation back then, because meditation meant sitting cross-legged with a straight back, with attention focused on my mantra.

I saw meditation in much the same way most beginning meditators see it: When I was doing the meditation instructions, even unsuccessfully, I was meditating. When I wasn't following a prescribed set of instructions—when I was letting my mind do as it pleased—I wasn't meditating. Since there was no one to give me the kind of guidance I now give students, I didn't know that what I was experiencing lying on my back could become the basis for a viable meditation practice. That wasn't meditation, and what was supposed to be meditation wasn't working for me, so I dropped it altogether for a number of years and for the most part forgot that

I could keep my body still for an hour or two and have my mind settle down and enter into a world of imagery.

In my early twenties, I tried other forms of meditation that came out of reading books on Tibetan Buddhism, but I soon realized that I needed to learn them from a teacher. I went to Nepal with the intention of pursuing a spiritual path but found myself teaching English instead. It was hard for me to connect with the Tibetan teachers, devotees, and teachings I encountered there, but I am glad I tried.

One day during our time in Nepal, my wife and I decided to go with a friend to a Tibetan nunnery in the foothills where a venerated lama was speaking. We hiked past a Vipassana meditation center on the way up to the temple, and *a few hundred yards* up the road I picked up a piece of paper lying on the ground. It was one of the center's brochures. I read it as we walked up the hill. All it contained was the daily schedule, which consisted of several hours a day of meditation, and the rules for a retreat, which were quite strict. I thought that if I went to that Vipassana center for ten days, I would surely get a serious meditation practice and would then be able to realize my spiritual aspirations for this life.

I called up the center, which taught the meditation method of the Indian Vipassana teacher S. N. Goenka, and enrolled in the next ten-day retreat, which was only a couple of weeks away. I recall trying to meditate on my own in preparation for the retreat, going back to using a mantra mostly, but without much success. I reckoned that when the retreat rolled around, I would really learn how to meditate.

The retreat began in the evening with meditation instructions. I sat in a full lotus position on a flat cushion. The meditation hall was a cement building. The floors were cold and hard, as there was no carpeting. I did as instructed. I brought my attention to the tip of my nostrils and noticed the sensations of my breath moving in and out. It was easier to feel the breath go in at first, but after a few minutes, I could detect the air brushing past my nostrils and upper lip, however faintly. My breathing started to speed up, making it easier to notice. I was surprised when the bell rang.

The next day we got up at around 4:00 A.M. and began sitting at 4:30. Once again I sat in full lotus, and as soon as I put my attention on my nostrils, my breathing quickened. I stayed focused on one breath following another for the next two hours. I remember seeing an image of a man in one of those heavy metal diving suits. He was floating deep underwater with barnacles all over the suit, as if he had been there for ages. I quickly interpreted that image as referring to an aspect of myself that was still unconscious, as I was fond of Jungian psychology at that time. But I was able to let go of such thoughts easily and keep my attention fastened on my breath.

A couple of days later, we were asked to switch from observing the breath to focusing on bodily sensations. On that day we were given instructions to scan our bodies from the top of our heads to the tips of our toes. This was done in a slow manner, taking about ninety minutes to do it completely. I found that I could also do that practice with good concentration, and after a few days I began to experience a free-flow of sensations up and down my body, which was what was supposed to happen when doing the practice consistently over the course of a retreat. I felt adept at that way of meditating as well. Here I had learned two new meditation techniques that I could do well.

I had found my meditation practice for life, or so I thought. After the retreat it was so easy to follow the meditation instruction to just notice the breath at the nostrils. There was hardly any thinking, my mind rarely wandered away from the breath, and my awareness of the air moving in and out of my nostrils was also soft and gentle. There was no force involved. There was harmony between my mind as it was and the instruction I used. I not only wished it would last forever but actually thought it would.

In the spring of the following year, my wife and I left Nepal, where we had lived for nearly six years, and went to Sri Lanka. As soon as we were off the plane and through immigration, we took a bus to Colombo and then another bus to a meditation center we had heard about. By nightfall we were receiving meditation instructions from one of the monks. Then we were separated. She was assigned to a small room in the female compound, and I was given a room on the outskirts of the monastery.

We had both done several ten-day meditation retreats in Nepal and India at centers teaching Goenka's Vipassana method. This meditation center taught the Vipassana method of the famed Burmese monk Mahasi Sayadaw. We were asked to stop doing Goenka's Vipassana. We were instructed not to observe our breath at the nostrils but instead to observe the rise and fall of our abdomen. We were instructed to note each sense impression in terms of the sense door (such as "hearing, hearing" for when we heard the sound of a bird, and not "bird chirping"). Also, we were told that we should alternate our sittings with one-hour periods of walking meditation, and we were given instructions to keep our attention focused on the lifting, moving, and placing of our feet as we slowly paced up and down the wide corridors.

Rather than unlearning our previous meditation practice, we were asked to abandon it and take up a new one—as if that were humanly possible. What I did was practice Goenka's method for about half the sittings during the day and then tried out the new method in the remaining sittings. I really didn't want to give up my familiar practice, even though instead of making me calmer and clearer, the moving of sensations up and down my body, along with alternating between sitting in lotus and half-lotus postures, was creating muscle tightening and spasms. Much of each sitting was taken up by painful sensations shooting through my body and the desire to relieve all the physical tension. Only in the early morning or after the midday meal did I feel relaxed enough to make it through an entire sitting without moving. I stuck with sitting through my pain and soon was able to devote more meditation sittings to this new method, and I began to have experiences that are common when practicing that method seriously and exclusively.

By the end of three weeks, I had decided to become a monk, and my wife had decided to become a nun. I ordained at that very same meditation center, while she left soon thereafter for Bodhgaya, India, since women weren't ordained at that center. I continued to meditate using the Mahasi method, trying to leave my old meditation practice behind, though I would often find myself focusing on my breath at the nostrils and, occasionally, moving sensations up and down my body.

Eventually I discovered ways to transition more thoroughly to what I saw as a more grounded and sensible meditation practice, which integrated the instructions of both methods, and which also helped me tolerate my physical discomfort. Instead of moving sensations through my body intentionally, I began to allow my attention to go where sensations emerged naturally, as is taught in the Mahasi method. Without the intention to move sensations, I found that sensations just popped up in places, sometimes in the same place over and over again. Whereas before I would become involved in having a sensation that formed in my head move down into my chest and abdomen, I was now just allowing the sensation to form as it would naturally in my head, remaining open to seeing what would happen. Often what happened was that I would become focused on the particular sensation and I would start to break it down into smaller pieces, or I would try to find the center of the ache or pain and concentrate on it. I could easily have picked these instructions up from a teacher, as I have heard these instructions since, but none of my teachers or fellow monks ever mentioned going into physical sensations in these two ways. In the strict Mahasi method, you were supposed to note each sensation as it arose and passed away, which works fine for fleeting sensations but not so well when something sticks around for a long time, especially if it gets worse. So I had to learn other ways to be with what I was naturally experiencing.

Another thing I discovered was that by bringing my attention to the contact of my ankles and rear sitting on the hard, cold cement floor of my room, I could learn how *not* to focus on bodily sensations. This was completely opposed to concentrating on the sensations. By having my attention on the external contact of sitting on the cold, hard floor, I could then experience internal sensations with a certain distance. I no longer got involved in either moving sensations or focusing intensely on them. The world of internal sensations, which, for me, were mostly dull pains, feelings of tightness, throbbing, vibrations, and tingling, seemed to become looser, freer, more dynamic and changing as I continued to sit in this way. Also, quite contrary to my expectations, I developed greater tolerance for painful sensations by not focusing on them.

During this period, a fair percentage of my sittings were dedicated to being aware of my breath, and I would often switch to awareness of breathing when there were periods of almost no physical pain. I wanted to switch my focus of attention on the breath from the nostrils to the abdomen, and that took some time and considerable patience. I just couldn't hold my attention on my belly for more than a few minutes. I would note "rising, rising" and "falling, falling" each time I felt my belly fully extend and contract, but it wasn't the same as noticing the touch of the breath at the nostrils, which came so easily for me. It had a forced quality to it. Most of the time, I was trying too hard to keep my attention on my abdomen. Something had to change.

What I did was apply the same principle I learned from sitting with sensations. Instead of trying to focus on my abdomen, I brought my attention to my whole body sitting still, and from that vantage point, I noticed what was moving. What was moving when I breathed naturally was not my abdomen but my diaphragm, chest, and collarbone. The movement was occurring higher up in my body. To make my abdomen move in and out required an intention to create that movement; in a sense, I had to change the way I breathed to become aware of the rise and fall of the abdomen. What I did instead was just breathe naturally, and having my attention on my whole body sitting still made that possible. I could follow my breath easily for most of the sitting if I wanted to.

But observing my whole body breathing was never as absorbing as observing my breath at my nostrils. Upon reading the Buddha's description in the Satipatthana Sutta (Discourse on Establishing Awareness) about bringing one's attention to the front of one's face and then noticing the breath go in and out, I tried that approach. It's basically the same principle as being aware of your diaphragm going up and down as you keep your attention on the still posture of sitting. Having my attention on my whole face, which was essentially still for the whole sitting, provided a way to be with and notice the air that moved out of my nostrils and into them.

As I became more established in being aware of my body sitting still, other things that had previously been excluded from my meditation practice began to become more prominent. I began to have longer periods of thinking. Emotions emerged in my thoughts, and I would feel them less as bodily sensations and more as moods, attitudes, eruptions of feeling. My mind would drift off into some hazy, drowsy, and yet very tranquil states for long stretches of time, sometimes lasting a couple of hours. I had successfully unlearned the meditation instructions I was taught. I was moving in the direction of allowing my mind to be as it was in meditation.

I intuitively knew that this was a truly remarkable and beneficial development, but from the standpoint of the meditation instructions I had learned, it didn't look that way. But this is how unlearning meditation looks, at least initially, both as a practice for beginners and as a direction for those who have learned a meditation practice.

2

Gentle Intentions

The limb of the Buddha's eightfold path that deals with intentions expressly states that two types of intention to develop in one's practice are those of nonharming and not killing. These are intentions to be gentle and kind.

We are not used to things changing through being gentle and kind, thinking that we must take decisive action or discipline ourselves with harsh methods (which include punishment and/or shame). There has to be some kind of faith or trust in the efficacy of gentle intentions to produce changes, for it doesn't make rational sense that by being kind and patient, and by essentially doing less, we will transform in significant ways. We tend to prefer direct approaches to change, such as working hard on one thing or taking a prescribed course of training. Something indirect, such as being gentle and allowing with one's inner experience, doesn't meet the rational requirements, doesn't suit the belief that change comes about by doing something that aims directly at what needs to be changed.

The third kind of intention the Buddha speaks of is the intention to renounce. It too is a soft intention, but it is often practiced in a strong, determined way that is not soft at all. What you renounce while unlearning meditation is not any previously learned meditation technique but, rather, any strong intentions that may have been attached to the technique. It becomes possible to do the meditation practices with gentle intentions. If you've learned, for example, to follow the breath as a meditation practice, this approach isn't about abandoning that practice; rather, it's about doing it without a strong intention. An example would be if you find yourself noticing the breath and you are able to gently focus your attention for a short while, seeing if it will stay there naturally or not. If your attention doesn't stay with the breath, then let it move to where it will. But if it does, you will be with the breath and experience the benefits of that practice, even though your attention may only stay there for a minute or so.

Loosening around the Instructions

The tension between *the meditation instructions you use* and *your mind as it is* in meditation leads to tightening or loosening around the instructions. When we tighten around meditation instructions, we try to do them exclusively, rigidly, "correctly." When we loosen around meditation instructions, we do them loosely, partially, or not at all.

There can often be a tightening around an instruction when you first learn it. It can't be helped. That is what we do when we receive instructions and try to do them correctly. We don't follow an instruction with the intent to be loose with it, for that would open the door for failure, for forgetting the instruction, for doing something other than the prescribed practice. No, we tend to want to do the instruction well, even perfectly, and get all the promised benefits from it.

The problem here is the type of intention that is required to do the instruction. To pursue this with you, I would have to propose that you consider that there are two types of intention to be found in the meditation instructions themselves:

- Strong, harsh, rigid intentions
- Gentle, light, flexible intentions

What tends to happen to you when you hear a meditation instruction such as "Be aware of your breath; when your mind wanders, bring it back to the breath" is that you have a strong, harsh, rigid intention to do just that. There is no room for doing anything else. The sole purpose of meditation becomes keeping your attention on the breath at all times.

What happens when that instruction becomes gentler, friendlier, more allowing? Say the teacher phrases it as, "Be aware of your breath. When your mind wanders, gently lead it back to the breath." Is that going to create a gentle intention instead of a harsh one? In my experience, it does not. In fact, it tends to set up a bind. You are still being told to disregard thoughts and to concentrate on the breath. Paradoxically, until there is a true allowing and acceptance of thoughts in meditation, it is unlikely you will learn how to gently disengage from thinking. The imperative to pull yourself out of each mind-wandering goes against the conditions that would lead to gentleness.

If you have been following the grand theme of the tension between *the meditation instructions you use* and *your mind as it is,* you will see that any instruction that asks you to concentrate on one part of your experience (the breath) and exclude other parts of your experience (thoughts) will set up an internal struggle when the two are in conflict (such as fighting off thoughts to stay with the breath). You could say that the purpose of learning the practice to be aware of the breath is to conquer the mind's own natural wildness and bring it in line with the breath. A struggle with *your mind as it is* occurs from the very outset by disallowing mind-wandering.

Long ago, having realized this and other problems with the instruction of following the breath, I decided not to teach meditation using it. Awareness of the breath is something I see people come to some time down the road on their own, when a good deal of harshness and rigidity has been weeded out of their meditation practice. Then it can be accomplished gently and effortlessly.

What I teach people new to meditation is to start with an awareness of the body sitting still. But it is hard to begin with an awareness of your whole body. So I ask them to start with bringing their attention to the touch of their hands on top of each other in their lap. The idea is not to hold your attention there all the time but to allow thoughts and feelings into the sitting also.

During the meditation sitting, anything that happens is okay. Falling asleep, planning a trip, worrying about a relationship, fantasizing, daydreaming, problem solving, anything. Wherever your mind goes, whatever comes up, however you feel, it is all okay. If you forget to notice your hands touching for a long period of time, that is fine too. All that is required of you is to sit still, but if you need to move, do so, and then resume a still posture. Your eyes can be closed or open, though I often find that this practice is more effective with eyes closed.

This may sound too loose to be a legitimate form of meditation. If your idea of meditation is staying with a particular object of meditation throughout the sitting, then this certainly doesn't count as meditation. And that is part of what can keep people from embarking on the path of unlearning meditation: it does not meet the commonly held views about what meditation is. The practice of unlearning meditation is, very simply, being with your experience of meditating. It is not about the meditation instructions, but about what you experience in meditation. The chart below can be used to compare instruction-centered meditation practices and this approach of unlearning meditation.

Traditional Meditation	Unlearning Meditation
Strong intentions	Gentle intentions
Focused on a prescribed object (e.g., the breath)	Grounded on the body sitting still while allowing anything to come up
Constant reminding oneself to return to the breath	Periodic remembering to return one's attention to the body or just finding

	one's attention on the body of its own accord
Judging oneself for doing the meditation practice wrong and trying to find the correct way of doing it	Being okay with how one is meditating much of the time, except for periods of doubt and confusion as to this being an acceptable way to meditate
Discipline in terms of staying with the task is important	Developing tolerance for difficult feelings, thoughts, and memories coming up is important

Not only is the orientation different, so is the way it is taught.

In my workshops I ask people to take a few moments after each sitting and try to call back to mind what they can remember from it. Often they can remember only a few things. So I suggest that you start with what you remember most easily and then try to recall things that are less clear. You can write down your recollections in a notebook or journal. Recollective Awareness Meditation gets its name from this feature of recalling and journaling sittings. The purpose of the recollection is to become familiar with your experiences in meditation. I will go into this in more depth later on, but for now what you need to know is that we can use our memory to cultivate present-moment awareness. It is generally believed by those who teach and practice mindfulness meditation that present-moment awareness (mindfulness) is developed by using techniques that bring one into the present moment. That is a direct approach to achieving the aim of being in the present.

Recollective Awareness is an indirect approach that accomplishes the same thing, but instead of only learning how to be present with the breath and bodily/sense experience as in the mindfulness techniques, one learns to be present with emotional and mental states, for that is what is often recalled. By recalling what you were experiencing emotionally in the meditation sitting afterward, you become more able to stay with similar emotional experiences when they arise again. And not only that, but you also become more interested in them and skilled in exploring them.

An important part of Recollective Awareness Meditation for many people has been talking about their meditation experiences with a teacher. Since some readers of this book may not have access to a teacher, I am including stories from individuals who have been meditating in this way, along with some actual journal entries from their sittings, including my observations and comments. I hope that you will be able to relate to some of what people have gone through and use that to further support your meditation practice. And you could always decide to attend one of my workshops or retreats, or those held by teachers I have trained.

Listed below are the basic meditation instructions for Recollective Awareness Meditation.

- Find a quiet spot to meditate where you most likely won't be disturbed by others or by the phone. Decide how long you are going to sit (anywhere from ten to forty minutes) and either set an alarm or have a clock nearby to peek at on occasion.
- Sit in a comfortable posture, one that you feel you will not need to change for the duration of the sitting, either on a chair, on a couch, or on a meditation mat or cushion. But if you do need to move during the meditation sitting, try to move slowly and quietly into a more comfortable posture.
- Close your eyes and bring your attention to the touch of your hands resting one on top of the other in your lap. But don't hold your attention there. Instead, allow your mind to go where it will. If you are drawn into thoughts, feelings, memories, or fantasies, let your attention go there. Your attention may at times also be drawn to sounds, bodily sensations, fragrances or odors, or your breath.
- When you feel that you have been away from the contact of your hands for several minutes, you can remind yourself to come back to the hands and stay there for a few seconds before allowing your mind to wander again.

- If you feel restless, bored, confused, discouraged, elated, sleepy, upset, anything, it is okay. You don't have to do anything about it, or you can bring your attention back to the touch of your hands. But if you do, just stay with your hands for a little while, and then if your mind wants to go back into the feelings or thoughts that you left, you can let it go there. If something else draws your attention, you can let it.
- When the meditation sitting is over, take a couple of minutes to mentally recall what you can of the sitting. You may also decide to journal your meditation sitting.
- And, you don't have to meditate every day.

Instructions for Journaling

- Before writing down the sitting, write down the date and time that the sitting took place. This is helpful when referring back to the journal entry.
- There are two basic ways to begin writing it down: to make a list or to write a narrative. If you decide to make a list of the events you recall from the sitting, I suggest that you use longer descriptions than single words. You don't need to write down the sitting in chronological order. You can start with what you remember most easily, and once you have that on paper, you can write down the other things that start to come to mind from the meditation. For those who like to have journal entries in chronological order, you can always rewrite the journal entry afterward, putting it in order, or mark entries in some way to give a picture of when they occurred.
- Your descriptions do not have to be exact. They just need to be truthful. If a description doesn't feel accurate, that is fine, as long as you are being honest. We can't hold ourselves to a high standard of precision and accuracy in this endeavor.
- Try to keep your journal entries focused on what went on during the meditation sitting. In the course of writing things down, you might have some thoughts about an experience.

You may write down your afterthoughts, but mark them in a way that shows they did not occur in the sitting (such as by putting them in parentheses).

- You will remember only a fraction of what goes on in many of your sittings. That is perfectly normal. Just write down what you can recollect. That is enough. Some journal entries may be many paragraphs long, while others may just have a couple of sentences.

Below are examples of narrative and list forms of meditation journaling.

Sunday, August 6, 2006   8 A.M. to 9 A.M.

Many thoughts about office space, buildings, leases, etc. Not really lost in the thoughts, or only for brief moments. Started to think that I wanted to know what to do about all of these things in a different way—not necessarily via thinking and weighing options. This thought led to a further distance from the thoughts, a closer, more dispassionate viewing. This was accompanied by a slowing down in thoughts, and then I noticed the orange-yellow light glowing behind my eyelids, and the tracking of my thoughts slowed to one at a time rather than in overlapping multiples. My awareness also began moving to my breathing at regular intervals. Started to think about how I'm growing very comfortable with my thoughts/thinking, not as frantically paced as they have been in the past, more floating, sometimes dancing lightly from one to the next—I felt at ease and peace with the thoughts and the process—same thoughts as in the beginning of the sit, all the practical day-to-day stuff—smiling.

1. Thinking about leasing office space, only lost in the thoughts briefly
2. Wanting some other way to handle these things, not by thinking about them

3. Felt more distant from the thoughts, more dispassionate
4. Saw an orange-yellow light
5. My thoughts slowed down to one at a time
6. Became aware of breathing at regular intervals
7. Felt at ease with the thoughts and the process
8. Ended the sit smiling

More Creative Ways of Journaling

For some people, writing a narrative or making a list of experiences just doesn't do justice to their meditation sittings. Also, sometimes writing about experiences in linear fashion presents problems, and a more creative approach is needed. Below are examples from two sittings by a student who is a graphic artist.

I suggest that you journal at least five meditation sittings. They do not need to be consecutive.

Wednesday night sangha sit

Had a new sensation of body & thought experienced as the surface of water. A dappled surface moving & broken. I was observing but also part of this pattern which was both internal & external.

Something like that

3

Instructions as Rules

Meditation instructions are, in many instances, a set of rules. At least that is how we tend to take them. We experience them more like orders to "meditate this way" than as directions on how to meditate skillfully.

Sometimes meditation instructions come to us with the rule explicitly stated: "Don't let your back slump. You must always sit with a straight back." How does this instruction feel to you? For some it might feel easy and effortless, making meditation much more accessible. But I fear that for many it will feel like a difficult task, one that requires great willpower and effort. Regardless of how it feels initially, in the meditation sitting itself, following this instruction will populate the sitting with reminders to keep the back straight, and you will continually correct your posture whenever you slump. And these reminders, intentions, and corrections will be a prominent feature of your experience of meditating; your feelings of success and failure may depend on how straight your back is throughout the sitting.

Other instructions have the rule implied in them, and whether you get the rule or not may depend upon how the instructions are initially delivered and reinforced over time. "Be aware of the breath" is a good example of this. Much of the time it is presented with the rule explicitly stated alongside it: "When your mind wanders, return to the breath." But sometimes it is delivered without the rule: "As you sit, you will notice your breath moving in and out at the nostrils. Try to stay with it." Here there isn't the rule to return to your breath when your mind wanders, but then again, you could interpret "Try to stay with it" as implying "Don't let your mind wander."

A rule forms whenever an instruction is stated as "You should do this, not that" or "When this happens, always do that." Rules function as preselected choices. When operating with a rule in mind, you don't have to consider the various other choices, for you tend to make your choice in accordance with the rule. Many meditation practices actually teach people not to make any other choice with certain experiences than the choice that is found in the instruction. In that way, meditation instructions limit our choices, though we may agree to that limiting quality because we often believe that the choice the instruction gives us is the best possible choice.

Sometimes teachers develop their own meditation instructions in response to the rigid, rule-based form of the instructions they were taught. So you might receive a meditation instruction to focus your attention on the breath and to accept other aspects of your experience at the same time. The instruction might read something like, "As you attend to the breath, you can also be aware of sounds, your body posture, bodily sensations, and your thoughts. Just note your thoughts as past, present, or future, letting them come and go." Now, on the surface this seems to resolve the problem of being aversive toward one's thinking in meditation, providing harmony between observing the breath and the other aspects of your experience. You are instructed to have a broader, more accepting stance toward your experience while, at the same time, you are training your attention to stay with the breath. Sounds perfect.

Then you try it out. First off, you will probably find that you can do only one instruction at a time. You pick the clearest, most definite one first. You observe the breath. How do you do that? By holding your attention on the breath and disallowing your thoughts, for thinking is usually a distraction from paying attention to your breath. Then, at some point, you may recall that you were going to be more accepting of your thoughts, sounds, bodily sensations, and so forth, and you let your attention leave your breath. All is well and good if you are calm and settled and able to do this. But if you're not able to do it, you find yourself going back to the breath and once again disallowing thoughts. The principle I would like to illustrate here is that the instruction to observe the breath will generally trump all other instructions given along with it, especially those instructions that contradict the instruction to stay with the breath. Such contradictory instructions often leave us either in a bind as to which one to follow or put us in a situation where we have to choose one over the other.

It may not always be the words we hear in the meditation instructions we receive but the tone of voice or feeling behind them that convey how the instruction is to be done. Certainly if you hear the instructions in a gentle, soothing, slightly hypnotic voice, you most likely won't notice if there is any harshness or contradiction in them—that is, until you do them without being under the influence of that soothing tone of voice. Some people get comforted and inspired by the voice in the instructions they receive and feel they must listen to recordings of instructions in order to do them. This is one way that the rule-based rigidity of many instructions gets past us.

The instructions for unlearning meditation are neither rigid nor contradictory. Like any instructions, they can be interpreted as rigid and used in a strict, inflexible manner, but that is definitely not the idea. I convey to students from the beginning that any experience they have in meditation is fine. There are no exceptions. Thus there are no contradictions. I do not say "Accept everything" and also "Focus on the breath" or anything of the sort. In fact, I would not say "Accept everything," for I believe that is unrealistic and impossible to do much of the time. Neither would

I instruct anyone to practice "choiceless awareness," because our experience is punctuated with necessary choices, and so to imagine functioning without choices seems incomprehensible.

Behind the Instructions

Now we are moving away from the subject of experiencing the instructions as rules to what is operating almost invisibly behind most of the instructions we receive. Meditation instructions also contain beliefs on the true nature of experience, the ways things truly are. I could state this as another proposition: embedded in the meditation instructions are concepts that are believed to be true and valid by the person giving the instructions (and, subsequently, by those who practice those instructions ardently). Most of the time we welcome this integration of practice and theory, primarily doing a particular meditation practice to arrive at the realization or a deep understanding of the concept(s) embedded in it.

So it may be difficult to see this as a problem or as something to be unlearned. If you are practicing meditation to be in the present moment, then why would you want to unlearn the concept of being in the present moment? Besides, if you have a belief that enlightenment is just being in the here and now, and you have no desire to question that belief, then it will feel perfectly correct and sensible to have that concept embedded in your meditation practice. You would never question its validity, its usefulness, or any of its qualities. You would just meditate in the appropriate ways to realize it.

It is not my wish to convince you otherwise. But it is my responsibility to help you see how concepts function in your meditation practice. I will be doing this at points throughout the book, so don't worry about my getting too involved in something that at the moment may sound abstract and metaphysical. It is really quite practical.

The way I see it, when looking at how concepts function in meditation, the issue of whether the idea is true or not doesn't matter. So it doesn't really matter whether being in the present moment is true enlightenment; we can still use it as an example of how concepts function in meditation instructions and our application of them.

A person sits down to meditate and brings her attention to the in-breath and the out-breath at her nostrils. She has been told that when she is exclusively with each in-breath and out-breath, she is in the present moment. Air enters her nostrils; she feels it pass into her head but does not follow it down to her lungs; a moment passes, then air moves up from her lungs and into her head, and after it passes through her nostrils she feels it brush against her upper lip. Each discrete part of this process is experienced as it is happening, which must be the case for it to fit into the concept of the present moment. Otherwise, parts of her experience would not be in the present, but in the past or the future. What parts of her experience would that be? Anticipating the breath making contact somewhere as it goes in and out, that would be looking toward the future, while recalling the touch of the breath once it is gone would be in the past. There is no leeway here; the present moment cannot be the past nor the future—it is strictly those times when one is with the touch of the breath.

Now let's step back a little and get a broader picture as to how this concept is functioning in relation to the instruction the meditator is following. As per the nature of concepts, it gives order and reason to the instruction. She is not just being aware of her breath without rhyme or reason—her awareness of her breath brings her into contact with the present moment, which is something much greater and more significant than just sitting and knowing that you are breathing. The concept creates a bridge from the mundane to the sublime.

But wait, that is only part of the story. The concept also divides her experience according to its logic. It agrees with the touch of the breath but not with her anticipation or recollection of the breath, so it must relegate those moments of memory and expectation to its opposite, the concept of not being in the present moment. How can you have being in the present without its opposite of not being in the present? Such concepts only come in pairs.

Then in meditation, it becomes customary to see one's experience in terms of mindful and unmindful, present and not present, self and no-self, to name but a few of the common concepts we learn when we take up a meditation practice. Under the surface of our experience, we are using these concepts to sort our experiences into acceptable and unacceptable, right and wrong, real and illusory.

And this brings us back to meditation instructions as rules. When the concept we have of meditation is to always be in the present moment, then it is quite natural to give birth to a rule that prohibits us from not being in the present moment. What is then prohibited or frowned upon in our meditation sittings happens to be our thoughts, feelings, memories, plans, and the like, all of which are subsumed under the category of not being present.

Now, if you have meditated without the concept of being in the present moment, then the concept of not being in the present probably wouldn't have appeared either. Your meditation sittings would not have that concept (and its opposite) embedded in it, so you probably wouldn't even be thinking about it. You wouldn't be judging yourself for not being present. You wouldn't feel you had to do things to yourself, change things about yourself, learn new meditation techniques in order to be present. You would be meditating for other reasons.

Are there any ways of meditating that do not have such concepts? I would have to say, all meditation practices, including what I teach, will have concepts embedded in them, and those concepts will be used as supports for the creation of rules on how one should be meditating. The only way to address this area of concepts in one's meditation practice is to go through a process of unlearning meditation. By looking into the concepts supporting your meditation practice, you may begin to disentangle yourself from ones that no longer work for you.

4

Unlearning for Beginning Meditators

Those of you who are just starting out on a meditation practice may wonder how all of this relates to you as a beginner. Let's say you are using the instructions found in chapter 2. There are a couple of places where you may take one of the instructions as a rule. You may turn the instruction to be aware of the touch of your hands into a rule that states you should try to always be with the feeling of the touch of the hands. That is not what the instruction actually says, but that is what we have usually heard when receiving instructions: our attention should always be directed on something. There really is no such rule stated in these instructions. Instead, you have the choice to go with whatever comes up for you, to bring your attention back to the touch of the hands on occasion, or to let your attention go wherever it is drawn (to the breath or to sounds, for instance).

If there is a rule in these instructions, it is this: "Try not to use strong, harsh, rigid intentions in your meditation sittings." That is true. These instructions are asking you to be receptive to what goes on without trying to control things. You are not encouraged to do a meditation practice where you are constantly bringing your attention back to your breath or your body, but you are not prohibited from doing it either. Such a prohibition would be a harsh, rigid intention.

There are also a few embedded concepts in my meditation instructions. The concept that most people comment on is the perceived emphasis on the mental world instead of the physical. Since most meditation instructions lean heavily toward being aware of bodily and sensory experience, and therefore often disregard or devalue mental experience, my instructions are often seen as more "psychological," giving far more attention to one's mental life. Of course, this view, which I do not share, perpetuates a view of the mind/body split that often accompanies teachings that primarily focus on the body and the senses. Granted, the instructions and approach do give more weight to the mental and emotional world than to the body, but please note that a key element of the instructions is to use your attention on the body as a base.

The instruction to allow your thoughts and feelings into the sitting has the view embedded in it that *your mind as it is* is potentially trustworthy in meditation. Meditation instructions that disallow thinking, reflection, or being open to the full range of experience usually imply a distrust of the mind. Some meditation students have expressed to me a fear of letting their minds wander too much in meditation. They fear that a wandering mind will open them up to negative thoughts, unwholesome feelings, uncontrollable urges; it may even lead to madness, depression, or demon possession (yes, I have heard that one more than once).

So, how are our minds trustworthy in meditation? That question can only be answered by having experiences of allowing thoughts and feelings into your meditation sittings and seeing for yourself if such an approach is actually trustworthy. I could try to convince you to trust your mind, but that would only lead to your trusting me about it. Trusting in something, or someone, is often a long process of getting to know a person in a variety of situations and finding that most of the time the person does things that are helpful, supportive, nurturing. It is the same with our minds in meditation. If after a period of getting to know your mind in meditation, it proves to do things that are helpful and beneficial, then it can become trustworthy.

The Concept of Dependent Arising

The most significant embedded concept in my meditation instructions, from the perspective of Dharma teaching, is "dependent arising," which is the Buddha's teaching that our experience is made up of causes and conditions and does not come about through a self, another being, God, or destiny. This complex teaching can be simply stated as, "When one thing arises, so does another"; nothing arises in isolation. Whatever suffering and joy we experience in our lives come about through causes and conditions, some of which we do not know. But we can begin to know more of how our thoughts and feelings are constructed by causes and conditions in our lives, and this approach to meditation helps add to our knowledge of this.

In the instruction to allow your thoughts and feelings into the meditation sitting, you are letting your inner world, and your outer life, into the meditation practice. Whatever is going on in your life will enter into your sittings, as will your customary ways of seeing yourself, others, and the world around you. Your inner world is not static either. You go from one experience to another, one feeling to another, one train of thought to another, following various associations that you make, directives that you give yourself, strategies that you devise, or you find yourself at times just receptively going with what comes up. In fact, as long as you are alive and sentient, something comes into your inner world and stays however long it will. And whatever arises is not coming up as an isolated entity but occurs in relation to other things. This is generally what dependent arising (conditions and causes) is in meditation.

But this embedded concept of dependent arising can get in the way of knowing how you actually see things if you take it as the way you must see things. For instance, if you don't see an experience as made up of conditions but see it as self, that is perfectly all right in this approach, because that is actually how you see it. In the same vein, if you believe in God, destiny, astrology, or any other system that explains causes and conditions for you, then I suggest you explore those accustomed ways of seeing your world instead of attempting to see your experiences from the point of view of dependent arising. By doing it this way, you can learn about the dependently arisen nature of the views you already possess.

5

Inconsistencies

You might have noticed, as I have, that there is a nagging incon-sistency in what I have been saying about meditation instructions and my own experience of following the breath that I told you about in the first chapter. When I began with the instruction to stay with the breath, I just stayed with it. My attention wouldn't leave it. I could say that the way my mind was in meditation and the meditation instructions worked in harmony. That focusing on the breath all the time does work. At least, it worked for me when I first got that instruction. I just reached a point where observing my breath didn't do anything more for me. This is not an uncommon situation for people who were able to do medita-tion instructions without any impediment or resistance to them but who then find themselves many years later having abandoned that practice.

There is a difference between unlearning a meditation practice you tried to do well, but couldn't, and unlearning one that you have done in an exemplary manner. Why would anyone want to unlearn a meditation practice that works for him? You might think that there must be certain conditions at work that make someone dissatisfied, disenchanted, or disillusioned with a perfectly fine meditation practice. Or maybe it is just time to move on?

During my prime period of watching the breath, I could notice each inhalation and exhalation for an entire hour-long sitting. After a few months of trying to keep up that kind of awareness in many of my sittings, I just lost interest. Bodily sensations would periodically come and dominate my experience, and I would go with them. Awareness of sounds, especially when I got into the Mahasi Sayadaw method, would draw me in, and I would notice the differences in each bird or insect chirping, as well as the man-made sounds of engines, radios, loudspeakers, and the like.

There was a slow, gradual shift as I moved through the Mahasi method, where I began questioning its philosophy, its psychology, and its system of interpreting experiences. I stopped naming my experiences and no longer directed my attention to any prescribed object of meditation. What was left? I could always return to the natural breath.

But I could also return to my body sitting. That began to intrigue me more than the breath. It was still, inert. I could just sit knowing the experience of sitting. There was nothing for me to make out of it.

But something unexpected did start to develop: I had thoughts and feelings, not just sensations and reactions (desire and aversion). You might have wondered where my feelings had gone during all of this meditation as a Buddhist monk. My wife was a nun in India and Nepal, and it was only when I began to truly allow my thoughts and feelings into my meditation sittings and didn't just try to note them or focus on them as sensations or breathe through them that I began to feel sorrow, loss, regret, and my own loneliness. I opened myself up to my anger, hurt, fear, and longing. I no longer believed I should not have such feelings. As I contemplated the teachings of the Buddha in Pali, I became more convinced than ever that having such feelings is essential for understanding his teaching. And sitting still with those feelings, I learned how to tolerate them and, eventually, how to quietly and gently explore them.

From this new orientation to meditation practice, observing the breath made no sense. Every time I thought of bringing my attention back to my breath I became aware that I was taking it away from a train of thought or a feeling that I needed to be with and learn how to look into. Breath meditation seemed to be in the service of my resistance to being with my feelings. It was no longer needed and was getting in the way. So attending to my breath left my practice. As did almost everything else I was formally taught.

Dropping a Meditation Practice That Doesn't Work

It might seem that it would be a simple and straightforward matter to abandon a meditation practice that was a struggle. And that as soon as something easier, friendlier, or just plain better for you came along, you could drop the old and embrace the new. Why this doesn't happen all that often goes to the heart of unlearning meditation. It is never a matter of simply dropping one practice and picking up a new one. There is an unlearning process to be gone through with each meditation practice we attempted to learn, even if we were not entirely committed to it.

Often when meditation instructions are given, they are given with the promise that if done correctly, you will experience a certain result. Some people are promised enlightenment, partial awakening, relief from stress or pain, greater concentration, happiness, bliss, peace of mind, an overall sense of well-being and accomplishment if they persist with the instruction and do it faithfully, ardently, consistently, and above all, correctly, as it is taught by the teacher or the lineage of teachers within a tradition.

This puts some meditators into a serious bind. Even though they may be having difficulty doing the instruction, if they stop doing it, they feel they won't realize the promise of the practice. They will have failed. The daily failures of not being able to do the meditation practice will pale in comparison with the monumental failure of never getting the promised outcome. Besides, everyone has heard stories of someone meditating for years and years in a certain way with no success, and then one day he gets it. All the struggle, turmoil, and pain has been of use. So it is quite common to think, "That can happen to me if I stick with this meditation practice long enough."

You may fail to reach what the teaching promises, but in truth, it is the meditation practice that has failed as a means to realize the teaching. You may be disappointed in yourself for giving up so soon, before the goal has been reached, but how do you know that just because others supposedly have reached this goal doing a particular meditation practice that the same would happen to you? You might arrive at a similar place through another practice, and you won't know it until you try another way. But if you keep pressing ahead with a practice that is not working, hoping that someday you will get it, then other opportunities are not tried.

Of course, there are many other factors that may keep you sticking with a practice that doesn't work or is difficult. The meditation instructions and the results ascribed to them may make such good sense as to appear irrefutable as the only way to meditate. You may also have had experiences doing a particular practice that are encouraging, even life changing, while at the same time feeling that you've not been doing it correctly or well enough. There is also the factor of your faith in the teacher, the tradition, or the religion supporting you in continuing with a set of meditation instructions that you might otherwise be inclined to give up. As you can see, there are these and other reasons why you might keep doing a particular practice. What about those factors that lead to unlearning that meditation practice?

One of the most powerful factors in the process of unlearning an existing meditation practice is your willingness to look honestly at that practice and how you've been doing it. To do this, you can't completely stop doing one practice and start doing another. You actually have to keep doing the one you've been doing. That is why I give the instruction to "meditate in the way you are accustomed to" to everyone who comes to me with an already existing meditation practice. Then I add, "You have permission also not to do that practice during the meditation sitting. You can try other meditation practices you have heard about, or you can try the beginning instructions I offer."

With these instructions, the choice is up to you what to do at various points in the meditation sittings. So sometimes you're meditating in your accustomed way, while at other times you can be experimenting with something different. What begins to happen is that your customary method is no longer the only way you meditate. It can be contrasted and compared with other practices you're doing. It has been bumped out of its privileged position of the only (or best) way to meditate.

Once again we come to the role of having more choices in meditation. But the idea here is not just to learn one practice after another, building up a repertoire of meditation practices that you can trot out whenever you like in your meditation sittings. It is simpler than that. Remember, this is about unlearning meditation, not learning a whole bunch of new techniques and strategies. The choices you may notice arising within your meditation sittings have to do with where to put your attention and what intention to follow.

For example, someone who has an existing practice of watching the breath might also begin to include meditating with awareness of his body. Say he was watching the breath exclusively in his sittings over a period of a few months and had sporadic success at holding his attention squarely on his breath for several minutes at a time. The rest of the time he found himself rehashing events of the day, which was unusually unpleasant and annoying for him, as the events were often conversations where he said the wrong thing. Now, as he sits with awareness of sitting, allowing his thoughts and feelings into his meditation, he notices that whenever he begins thinking about things he has said, he has a strong intention to bring his attention to the breath. In the past, he just thought he was faithfully following the instruction to return to the breath, but now he realizes that he was using the technique of watching his breath as a way to avoid being with his regrets and worries. With that glimpse into himself and how he was using the instruction to stay with the breath, he can now make the choice when a painful memory comes up whether to stay with it, tolerate it, and learn about it or to move away from it by going to the breath. Now there is choice where before there was just habit.

Having freedom of choice in one's meditation sittings is important for opening up meditation instructions to contrast and comparison, but it in itself cannot bring about unlearning. It is the looking into one's meditation practice that actually paves the way for unlearning meditation.

Bridges from Other Practices

In order to move into a more unstructured meditation practice, you may need to find a bridge that leads from your existing meditation practice to meditating in a more open, receptive manner. Such bridges can undo some of the work that was accomplished in your previous meditation practice, so there is often reluctance to use them once they are found or pointed out. But without using a bridge, you can find that instead of unlearning meditation, you've just adopted a new practice to replace the old one, and the new one may function very much like the old one.

For example, if you've practiced focusing on particular sensations with the idea of feeling emotions in the body, then you may need to find a bridge to once again experience emotions in your thoughts, as you most likely did before learning that technique. Such a bridge might be found by placing your attention on the mental mood that arises with the sensation. Another bridge may be to notice the tone of voice in your thoughts and, from that, learn to pick out the emotions within your thinking process.

You may wonder why you would need to unlearn experiencing emotions as bodily sensations. There are a variety of reasons. For one, emotions, such as fear, desire, hatred, and sadness, are usually experienced with accompanying images, impressions, and thoughts. When only the physical sensations of those emotions are focused on, the mental elements of the emotional experience get obscured and lost. What then happens is that you only notice emotions when they manifest physically. Along with that comes the notion that if you can just observe the physical sensations come and go, without becoming attached to them, the concurrent emotion will diminish, vanish, or be let go of.

By turning emotions into bodily sensations, you are turning them into another form. That is, you are transforming them. At first that seems like a good idea. It simplifies your emotional world. It concretizes emotions and can be used to control them. You can more easily try to detach from the sensations or, conversely, focus on them and go into them. But are these sensations really the same thing as emotions? They may be a significant part of your emotional experience, but they are not the whole story. By gradually reversing this transmutation of emotions into bodily sensations and becoming more acquainted with the thoughts, memories, and intentions that are also part of your emotional experience, you can become aware of the whole story or, at least, as much as you can know and handle at that time.

6

Putting Meditation Experiences into Words

When you put language to a meditation experience, do you use the terminology found within your tradition or meditation community or do you use your own words? Most meditators with a formal meditation practice tend to use the words of their tradition or community. The language we use to talk about what goes on in meditation sittings is often learned. Even people who have never meditated before or who have been meditating on their own with the help of audio recordings or books learn a particular way of referring to their practice and the experiences they have.

The type of language used in talking about meditation experiences is often conceptual, metaphorical, and abstract. Emotions are often put into broad categories, where rage, contempt, resentment, hatred, vengeance, and the like are all called anger. Thoughts are classified in terms that inevitably convey that they do not belong in meditation: *planning, monkey mind, distractions, past or future, fantasy, daydreaming,* and the common expression used in instructions, *mind-wandering.*

In Buddhist meditation practices, particularly Vipassana meditation, there is a tendency to use the Abhidhamma (Higher

Teachings) as the basis for how people should look at and talk about meditative experiences. The Abhidhamma is generally considered by scholars to have been composed a few hundred years after the Buddha's passing. The early Abhidhamma period focuses a good deal on the language one should use in discussing the Dharma (teachings of the Buddha) and makes a contrast between the "figurative" and inexact language used by the Buddha in his discourses and the precise terminology found in the Abhidhamma texts. As Venerable U Revata states in his introduction to Bhikkhu Bodhi and Mahathera Narada's translation of the *Comprehensive Manual of Abhidhamma:*

> The Buddha freely employs the didactic means required to make the doctrine intelligible to his listeners. He uses simile and metaphor; he exhorts, advises, and inspires; he sizes up the inclinations and aptitudes of his audience and adjusts the presentation of the teaching so that it will awaken a positive response.
>
> [Whereas the] Abhidhamma takes no account of the personal inclinations and cognitive capacities of the listeners; it makes no concessions to particular pragmatic requirements. It reveals the architectonics of actuality in an abstract, formalistic manner utterly devoid of literary embellishments and pedagogical expedients.

The Buddha will use common words, such as *person* and *self,* while the Abhidhamma describes inner experiences in terms of *elements* and their characteristics, relations, and functions. The Buddha uses a variety of words to convey nuances of experience, perception, and understanding, while the Abhidhamma systematically reduces the meanings of words so that they can fit into doctrinally relevant categories. Where the Buddha describes an experience with the aid of similes, metaphors, and unusual word choices, the Abhidhamma provides the student with a single-word concept of the experience and includes it within a categorical system of pairs, groups of three, and longer lists. It is a system that suits abstract thinkers and those who seek order within themselves.

The Buddha's Language

The Buddha used words, phrases, metaphors, and similes to talk about the meditative experiences he and others around him had. Some scholars believe that his original language was some form of ancient Magadhi, which was later combined with features of other neighboring languages and developed into the Pali language. Sometime later, the Buddha's expressions were put into a hybrid form of Sanskrit. Over the centuries, the Buddha's words have been translated into many Asian languages and, in modern times, into Western languages.

The Buddha chose to name, describe, and express meditative experiences in his own words, occasionally borrowing words from the other teachings of his day, using those words as a native speaker would. He didn't need to go to a dictionary, read divergent translations, or consult with learned pandits on the meanings and connotation of the words he chose, but that is what we have to do when we embark on learning his language. Our situation with the Pali language and the texts written in it is that we can only attempt to reconstruct what the Buddha meant when he said all those wondrous things, as there can be no one who knows that language as it was spoken and understood during his lifetime (especially considering that he spoke in a dialect that has essentially been lost to us).

This does not mean it is futile to try to understand those teachings. What it does mean, however, is that the language he used in talking about his experiences in meditation is not the language each of us uses today. Just as he used his own language to refer to what he experienced and understood, we must also use our own language, for it is through our native tongue (or a second language we have gained fluency in) that we may be able to independently name and describe our experiences and have little or no question about the meanings of the words we choose.

For this reason I have largely moved away from using Pali terms and their English equivalents in teaching meditation, though I sometimes use them in Dharma teaching, since in that context,

I am relating a teaching given by the Buddha and translating his language to the best of my knowledge. But when it comes to talking about our own inner experiences and how we understand them, language that rolls off our tongue and conveys our thoughts and feelings with greater certainty and clarity is far better than one that we are struggling to learn.

Drawbacks of Using Single Words to Describe Experiences

We often use the words *fantasy* and *daydreaming* to describe periods when we are lost in thoughts about what at first seem to be purely mental situations, such as rehashing a conversation and rehearsing a reply; working on the solution to a problem; writing an essay, story, or book; imagining a future scenario of wealth, happiness, or success; sexual thoughts and fantasies; or those periods when our minds just create some kind of unusual or nonsensical scenario out of thin air.

Noticing and talking about thoughts as "distractions," "past or future," or "monkey mind" often leads to a rejection and devaluation of one's thoughts in meditation. These terms are used to describe thoughts in relation to how they fit with the instructions and concepts of the meditation practice. In a practice of trying to watch the breath all the time, thoughts will most likely be experienced as distractions. If one is trying to be in the present moment with awareness of the breath, then most thinking will be either of the past or of the future, except for that thinking which is reminding one to be in the present moment or to return to the breath. And *monkey mind* tends to conjure up an image of a monkey running amok in one's head. I believe it is often used as shorthand for simply saying, "My mind is racing and I just can't control it!"

Words such as *planning* and *thinking* function like all of the above and, like the words you use for emotions, are the hardest to truly question, for you may seem to get close to what you're experiencing when using such words. But that is because you have not gone into fuller, detailed descriptions of what is going on when you notice yourself planning or thinking.

This brings up the whole area of not going into the content of your experience. *Planning* and *thinking* are general terms that are meant to indicate the process one is going through. But how can process be separated from content? When you try to look at thinking without noticing the content of the thoughts, the process of thinking (or act of thinking) becomes the object of your awareness and thus becomes the content of your experience. Meditators who practice noticing thinking as "thinking, thinking" may find that when they have been thinking for a period of time, they remember very little of what they were thinking about, for they have not been paying attention to the content. But they do recall that they were thinking.

In the language of Vipassana meditation, they were attending to the mind door of experience, where the mind is supposedly operating like any other sense door with its objects of awareness. Just as the eye sees shapes, the mind thinks thoughts. One need not bother with the content of the thoughts, for Vipassana meditators are mostly instructed to shift their attention away from sense objects to the sense doors. So they learn to be aware of the activity of thinking and tend to regard all thoughts as equally undesirable. Thus, not only is what one thinks about deemed irrelevant, but attending to it, especially staying with it and examining it (yet more thinking), is considered a wrong form of practice.

From the point of view of knowing, describing, and understanding your experience, what you are thinking about is as important as the process of thinking itself. In fact, the process of thinking may actually be affected by the kind of thoughts you are having. The same is true for planning. Say I am thinking about a particular person I am planning to meet after the meditation workshop is over and I am dreading seeing him, trying to figure out what I will say and do when I see him. When such experiences in meditation are described as just thinking or planning, there is really no knowledge of what was going on at that time, which, in this instance, was a period of dreading someone and figuring out what to say to him. But if you are asked what you were planning and give a description of the experience like I just did, then knowledge of what was going on in your mind can be recovered. This is where recollection can further your ability to know experiences that have previously been summed up by a single-word concept.

How We Talk about Physical Experiences

Meditation students are also generally instructed to talk about bodily experience using single-word descriptors. Sensations are hot or cold, sharp or dull, pleasant or unpleasant, vibrating or tingling. Your body feels light, heavy, porous, or spacious. The breath is coarse or fine, slow or fast, long or short, easeful or heavy.

This seems to be the appropriate way to talk about our bodily experience. When we go to the doctor, we report our sensations using these same descriptive words. But when we are asked to go further into a description of our bodily experiences, we may find that we lack a certain vocabulary and have to resort to similes: "The pain was sharp and spread like splinters."

The same holds true when writing or talking about physical sensations in meditation. We often have to get creative or recall useful similes in talking about them in any detail. As we do, we are also developing a finer sensibility around our bodily experience. An experience one might have previously described as "heavy" becomes "grounded and solid like a mountain." Such descriptions may sound as though you are moving away from the physical experience, but that is not really the case. The added adjectives and simile in this description can communicate effectively to both those who have had similar experiences in meditation and those who have not.

What I have said in this chapter relates to how language will be used when describing the experiences of meditators in this book. Instead of distilling people's experiences into single-word concepts of the experience or placing interpretations on them, I will try to present you with their experiences as they were related to me (or to themselves in their meditation journals). As you read their experiences, I suggest you refer to your own experiences in meditation (or similar ones outside of meditation) and use this material to reflect on what goes on in your meditation sittings.

7

Personal Stories

Many meditation practices that come out of the East discourage meditation students from paying attention to their personal stories in meditation while at the same time giving them stories about enlightened or awakened individuals. The emphasis is on learning the stories of the meditation practice or its tradition and using those historical figures and their experiences as models of higher development. The path and goal of meditation is sometimes stated as getting past your personal story, to transcend the ego. At the same time, your life history and concerns are often deemed somehow inferior, wrong, or deluded.

Yet Western psychology tends to value our personal stories, as do most of us. So when Eastern meditation practices with an ideology of transcending the ego collide with psychologically informed Western meditators, what tends to happen is that personal stories are axed from the meditation practice in the pursuit of finding a transcendent reality.

At first it does sound like a great idea to take a vacation from our worries, cares, complexes, obsessions, you name it, and bask on a sunny transcendent beach, lulled by each in-breath and out-breath or the hum of a mantra. Getting this taste of deep contentment on vacation, one naturally longs to move there, to merge with the transcendent One. "This is what Eastern meditation practice is really about," I think to myself for a moment, and then I recall how many times I have visited this vacation spot before, and each time I had to return home. And returning home was never easy, as I hadn't wanted to leave my vacation spot in the first place. I wanted to make it last forever. But, alas, it could last only as long as it would last.

The Buddhist practitioner steeped in Dharma teachings may have a different story about this experience from that of the transcendentalist I momentarily slipped into. As a Vipassana meditator, the sunny transcendent beach is right there in my attention staying with each in-breath and out-breath. "This is all there is," I tell myself, "I have no past nor future. Each moment is coming and going." Within the flux of one moment of awareness vanishing and another arising, there is no self to be aware of, no self that is in the awareness. It is pure awareness knowing the impermanence of all things. And when I return from this vacation, wishing that I could have stayed there forever, I am comforted to know that everything is changing, though I still hold on to that experience of impermanence as the true mark of existence.

The teacher of unlearning meditation now steps in and sees these two scenarios as stories about meditation, and personal ones at that. For some unknown reason, an acceptable story about meditative states, experiences, and realizations gets treated with greater validity and trust than your own, which is more honest and realistic. Do meditation students realize that they are trading in their personal stories of turmoil, growth, failure, fortune, and the like with the hope of arriving at someone else's attainment? It may not look like that at first, because it sounds like the person is just uprooting the ego and merging with the transcendent, which sounds perfectly acceptable. But wait! This transcendence happened to somebody, not to an abstract entity. This enlightened somebody was a human being, a story maker like the rest of us, and frankly, he composed a personal story about his meditative experiences that, incidentally, had various ingredients found in his tradition's stories of transcendence.

You might argue, and I might do the same, that the person was radically and permanently changed by the experience captured in his story, proving the truth of the transcendent experience and the validity of the story. Such proof has to be tested in the course of time. Since we can't get inside the person's head, we can't quite know what is going on there unless he tells us things. Those things he tells us are stories, though they may be couched as facts, truths, realities.

We may clutch these stories as the core of meditation practice in a chosen tradition, hoping that by remembering them, and applying their methods, we will touch the truth within them. To do that, we must then believe that the stories of enlightenment, of awakening, of higher states of consciousness, do rest on an experiential truth, which human beings are capable of discovering. There has to be something real that the stories help us get at. That truth is not the story composed about it. It is the experience.

Personal Narratives

Our personal stories, however, have a distinct ring of truth to them. They are experiential but not the bodily or sense-based experiences one learns to appreciate and value in meditation. Personal stories have a running narrative, themes, characters, beliefs, plots and subplots, in short, all the ingredients of a story. As such, they can be dramatic, funny, ironic, fanciful, or realistically descriptive. They are open to investigation and critical analysis, as one would find when recollecting one's narratives in a meditation sitting and writing them down. They tend to get replayed in our meditations and outside of them, and just like an endlessly repeated sitcom on TV, we enjoy the episodes we like and passively endure the ones we don't, or we just turn the channel.

So much time in meditation is taken up by our stories, so why not accept them into our meditation sittings? Why not let our internal narrators take the stage and perform? They will do it anyway, without asking our permission. And there may be things for us to learn about ourselves from enduring their performances.

I often suggest that meditators notice the narrator's voice, his or her speech patterns, the choice of words, and the emotional tone or flavor in the narration. The direction here is to move closer to who is doing the talking in your head. Is it your voice? Or are you using someone else's voice for this particular story?

Having a good idea of the narrator is one part of the equation. When we are narrating a story, we are talking to an audience. There is a particular someone, or a group of people, to whom the narrative is being directed. Your choice of words might give you a clue as to who that audience is. Another way to bring the audience out of the shadows and closer to the stage is to see this internal monologue as a performance for somebody, not just yourself. Maybe it is for somebody's attention. You want a particular person to hear this story, not just anyone.

Many narratives are not monologues. You might notice that you get into some pretty intense dialogues in your meditation sittings. Dialogues can be reruns of real conversations with different options and endings, or they can be completely new creations based on previous ones. They can also be debates, chitchat, or storytelling.

In the meditation journals I receive, people sometimes report having conversations with me in their sittings. By knowing that I will be reading their journals, they speak directly to me in them, setting up a dialogue in the journaling process. Rather than ignoring this relationship that is formed between a student and me, I tend to want to talk about it. The story of your relationship with your teacher is an important one, and I believe it needs to be looked at in the process of unlearning meditation.

Reality and Fantasy

This brings me to the whole issue of reality and fantasy in our stories. If our real stories are considered to be a waste of time in meditation, then a fantasy must be an even bigger waste of time. It is generally much harder for meditation students to tolerate having a fantasy in their meditation sittings than a reimagining of an actual past event. I generally prefer not to use the word *fantasy* when talking about imagined scenarios occurring within meditation sittings, for fantasies are looked down on by most meditation traditions.

In Western psychology, there is a history of looking at our fantasy lives and seeing what they can reveal about us, whether they are based on true events or imagined ones. Our imaginings are sometimes the very stories that perpetuate dissatisfaction with ourselves and others, being the burden that we carry with us. They are used to base our hopes and dreams on, and often, when unexamined, our concocted scenarios of the future are what we tend to follow. They can't just be eliminated by trying to stop our mind from going into the past and the future. Such stories are often too deeply embedded to be put to rest by finding some temporary way around them.

Meditation is a perfect place to sit with our stories and get to know them. They will come up often, so why not invite them in? With a growing tolerance of them and patience with the process of being with them, we may find it is not such a disagreeable way to spend part of a meditation sitting after all. It is quite possible, with the added quality of sincere interest in them, that we will find exploring them to be a valuable practice.

Which Story to Follow?

When meditating using one of the techniques that disallow thinking, the question about which story to follow doesn't come up. But when we let ourselves think about things in our sittings, we may want to have some criteria regarding which stories we should pay attention to and which ones should be passed over. This must be learned through trial and error, by taking a risk and following a narrative to see where it leads.

One predominant way of choosing which narrative to follow is to let the story choose you. That is, to simply follow whatever particularly holds your interest. These are often repetitive thoughts and feelings that you may feel you have already sat with enough or talked about enough or worked through completely. The sad truth is that nothing really gets worked through completely, and recurring themes in your life tend to emerge in meditation. So at first, when one of these themes or issues comes up, you may resist it and try to put your attention elsewhere. When you find that that's not working, you can just become aware of your feelings about wanting to avoid it. You don't have to go into it. And in fact, by focusing on your feelings about it, you will become aware of the narrative that causes you to avoid it. That narrative may be one of having worked through it or of having reached some other conclusion about it, such as that it is trivial and doesn't deserve any more attention. The narrative might sometimes be one of fear or shame. Eventually, from having stayed with and explored the narratives that keep you from being with this recurrent theme, you may find that you will be able to go into that theme without much resistance when it arises again.

We generally think that there is nothing to be learned from a mundane train of thought, such as making a list, reviewing a conversation, organizing something, or imagining a future event. Since these might not seem "juicy" enough narratives, we pass over them, usually by stopping such thoughts midstream in meditation. But I encourage you to explore them. What may start out as mundane (which is just a judgment placed on it without really knowing much about it) can turn into a train of thought that leads to something profound.

Generally, I recommend letting the themes emerge on their own in your meditation sittings instead of bringing issues into the sittings to look at. But occasionally people have told me that many of the most important issues in their lives never enter into their meditation sittings. Once they sit down, their minds go to other things, or get calm, and the big things going on in their lives don't come up. When that happens for you over a period of time, it might be useful to experiment with bringing issues into your sittings. The most effective way of doing this is to sit when you are in the midst of going through such an issue. That could mean that you would have to meditate at an odd time and in an unusual setting or that you would have to stop other things that you were doing. For instance, you might get into an argument with someone and want to sit with your feelings. Or you might realize something about a kind of unwanted behavior and sense that you are more connected with it at that moment and that it would be a perfect time to sit with it.

The Narrative of Recollection

Over the years I have received a wide range of feedback on the practice of recollecting meditation sittings, talking about them afterward, and writing them down in a journal. One of the main objections has to do with the "accuracy" of the narrative as it relates to the experiences. Some people gravitate toward a blanket statement that meditative experiences (or any experience, for that matter) can't be accurately conveyed with language. Some go to the other extreme, assuming that the language we use to describe an experience is capable of describing that experience perfectly.

One extreme places more weight on the truth and reality of words and ideas, while the other emphasizes the truth of experience. Most meditation teachings will propound the "truth of experience" view while at the same time placing significant weight on the truth of their words and ideas. So when I encounter a student who argues that all of this recollecting and journaling is removed from experience, I wholeheartedly agree. But after nodding my head in agreement, I will usually reply that we are putting language to our experiences anyhow, and the language we generally use may be even further removed from the experiences they are meant to describe than what we are putting down in our meditation journals. Longer descriptive phrases and clauses provide more information than single-word concepts. Of course, a description of an experience cannot be entirely accurate, but the fact is that we are either going to forget the experience entirely by not describing it or we are going to label it in a perfunctory manner, which in either case leaves us with an inadequate story about the experience. So, what I am asking you to consider here is that by recollecting the experience and putting it into your own words, you are actually less removed from the experience.

The journaling process brings with it its own problems. It can produce a certain amount of commenting on your experience and rehearsing what you will write. So some people journal about the thoughts they had regarding journaling and, on occasion, curse me for giving them this task to write down their sittings. As much as I would like people to be able to tolerate this side effect, I truly understand when it gets in the way and starts to dominate the meditation sitting. To alleviate this unwanted side effect, you can decide before or during the sitting not to journal afterward. After the sitting, however, you can open your journal and start writing, or you can follow through with your decision and not write about that sitting. Also, I don't recommend that you write down every sitting; it may be something you do only occasionally.

I'm often asked, "What do I do with my journal?" Keeping a journal is helpful for looking back over a period of meditation practice, either as part of your own self-review or as preparation for talking with a teacher about your sittings. When meditators don't keep a journal, their sittings can blend into a blur, with perhaps one key experience standing out. Then what generally happens is that people remember only certain significant experiences and mostly forget everything else they have gone through in meditation. When that happens, it is difficult to learn from your past sittings. Having a journal handy will aid your memory and, on occasion, prompt you to reflect on and ponder your meditation sittings.

As preparation for talking with a teacher, the journal provides a document that can be referenced during the interview. As you relate the sitting, either by reading the journal entry or by just glancing at it on occasion to jog your memory, new information about the sitting is often recalled. Then when the teacher asks questions about the sitting, there is the possibility that what was on the periphery of your awareness, and did not make it into the journal, may come out in the interview. The sitting becomes richer, and you can often learn things about yourself, and the meditative process, from this exploration of the sitting. And this kind of exploration can enter into your subsequent sittings.

8

Qualities

Various qualities are more readily developed through unlearning meditation than through other, more traditional practices. Unlearning meditation may actually be a trade-off for some people, where they change in certain ways they can appreciate and value, but not necessarily in ways they intended.

The qualities of mind developed in unlearning meditation are not necessary the same ones that are found in Vipassana, Zen, or Tibetan meditation practices. One who has studied the different Buddhist schools and their practices might also concur that the mindfulness developed in the Mahasi method is different from the spacious mind of Dzogchen; that realizing the meaning of a koan is not the same as exploring and inquiring into the nature of thoughts, feelings, perceptions, and sensations; and that observing each in- and out-breath is not the same kind of focused attention as focusing on a sensation and following the associations that come to mind.

Before reading on, you may ask yourself what qualities (or abilities) you have developed from the various practices you have done. Unlearning meditation is not going to take them away but, rather, will help you develop them in combination with other qualities. So if you have developed concentration from observing the breath, you won't lose that hard-won ability through unlearning meditation. You will, however, learn things about that type of concentration that makes it an asset in some situations, but not in others. By examining it more closely, you will be able to see the limitations and deficiencies of that kind of concentration and also its strengths. The same holds true for the mindfulness you might have developed, the discipline and effort you have applied, and the insightful understandings you have had. In the various practices you have done, those qualities have been developed in a certain way. I would hope you would find it pleasant, peaceful, and wholesome to add other qualities to them, allowing them to interact like new ingredients in a favorite recipe.

Tolerating Your Experiences

In most meditation practices, people are instructed to calm the mind before looking at intense emotional material. The calmness enables them to tolerate their emotions. But when they do that, the intense emotional material is no longer intense; it is muted, distant, ephemeral. Someone in such a state is generally quite content not to have the intense feelings anymore. The practice then turns into a way to get beyond emotional intensity, and into a calm state, instead of a way to look into emotions. The quality of mind that is being developed here is calmness.

Many people meditate just to arrive at a state of calm, so what is wrong with this picture? Nothing, if the purpose is to get calm and not experience any emotions. But if the purpose is to learn about intense emotions so that you can be less dominated by them, then there is something not quite right in always relying upon a quality that makes it impossible to look at them. The need to be calm in order to be with intense feelings may turn into a way to postpone being with such feelings. It may even lend support to the notion that being with such feelings is unnecessary as long as one can pacify them through meditation. The hard reality here is that intense emotions will keep popping up, sometimes when you least expect them, and you may find that the tools that worked to get you calm don't always work when you need them.

The way to be with an experience as it is involves the cultivation of greater tolerance for such experiences. We don't begin by tolerating intense, unacceptable thoughts and feelings in meditation. We start out wanting to manage them or get rid of them. That is understandable. And if certain techniques aid in that, naturally we try them out. But these techniques may get us calm instead of enabling us to build up enough tolerance for difficult experiences.

Developing tolerance is a gradual process. You can't force it. Forcing yourself to tolerate something that you feel you should be able to bear, like knee pain during meditation, often leads to a struggle with the pain and anger from being with it. The same is true of trying to tolerate emotions such as fear, rage, or grief. These difficult-to-tolerate experiences need gentleness, not force. We need to have patience with ourselves and not feel pressured to get through the discomfort.

Many of you who have been meditating for some time may just find that a little shift in how you relate to your thoughts and feelings in your sittings will facilitate becoming tolerant of them. Those of you who have begun with the instructions in this book may find that you have already made this shift without having to give it too much thought.

Here are a couple of journal entries from a longtime meditator who came to one of my retreats.

> First sitting: I noticed a shift in my practice today as I concentrated less on the breath and started to become aware of other things that were going on in my body. I noticed a ringing kind of static noise that was like sound but seemed to come from within my brain, between the ears. I have recently become aware that I tend to stop my mind from talking when it is midsentence and return to what I think is a meditative state. Today I intended to become more aware

of that before the meditation, and the result was a feeling of more allowing. I noticed that I tend to stop the thoughts when they are just about done anyway, so I just let them go more toward their conclusion. I always seem to have an abundance of erotic thoughts or imaginings, visions of naked girlfriends that come and go. I allowed these also. Toward the end of the meditation things seemed to become quite peaceful, and the time between thoughts grew large. A sense of peace and joy that was subtle and slight was with me, and I felt like I did not want to stop at the end of the half hour. I noticed that I was thinking about what I was going to write about during the meditation and I don't think I wrote about much of the things I thought about.

Second sitting: Neutral is a word that I would use to describe today's sitting, and it seems that same word describes my general feeling lately. There were no swings of emotion, and there was a sense of tranquillity. I am getting better at letting my thoughts go to their conclusion and then recognizing the space that is created between thoughts. A lot of planning goes on, yet the plans are not realized or acted upon after the sitting, so I wonder why I plan so often during sitting. It feels good to sit and do nothing, because it is the one time during the day when there are no demands upon me to act or be something. I feel very patient and understanding of the pace at which things change, which often seems slow.

In these sittings the meditator is not only noticing how he has stopped his thoughts as part of his previous meditation practice, he is also learning to tolerate their going toward their conclusion. Basically, the practice of cutting off your thoughts in midsentence or midscene does not cultivate tolerance for thinking in meditation but, rather, leads to its opposite. By allowing sexual fantasies and plans into his sittings, he finds that they too run their course, and he is not consumed by them for the remainder of the meditation, as one might fear, but instead his mind moves on to other things and to other states of mind. In this process he is also developing other qualities, such as patience with himself and the pace of his meditation and interest in understanding his planning mind instead of trying to find ways to stop it.

Of course, there are sittings from hell, which are exponentially more intolerable than the one described above. My advice to you is that if you are overwhelmed by an emotion, a scene, a type of thinking, or a memory, do not force yourself to stay with it. Be with it up to the point when you can't take it anymore, and then bring your attention to something grounding, like the touch of your hands or the breath or anything you've found to be a good anchor at such times. Just let your attention become grounded for a little while, and if the feelings, thoughts, or memories return, let yourself go back into them. You may have to go back and forth for some time in the sitting before you begin to notice a greater tolerance for the intense inner experience and, consequently, have less need to return your attention to something that grounds you.

In time you may then be able not only to tolerate such "horrendous" and "tumultuous" meditations, you may also begin to understand what keeps them going, as in this next journal entry. This is a different meditator, whose former practice involved labeling emotional experiences and distancing from them. After a few years of working with me closely, he has lost the distance and control over such intense experiences in favor of being in them and able to tolerate them to a high degree.

> I have avoided sitting the last couple of days. This follows several really good days with my girlfriend, and then we had a fight. Not really even sure what about. Felt put down, not good enough. Old bogeymen. Sat the night it happened, as I couldn't sleep. Poor night's sleep the night before, and waited until she left and then sat. Feel alive with sensation, heart pounding, guts churning, really don't want to sit. Initial thoughts of revisiting fight, her saying I am willing to settle for less, I accept being treated badly by staying at my job (she is a coworker), kind of rush of thoughts. Some anger, but I

think mostly sadness and fear. Back to thoughts around argument, maybe she is right, which I said in midst of argument, maybe I do settle and am willing to be put upon, maybe I will never change, her doubting me and whether she wants to be with someone like that. Painful thought of her in the morning asking me to leave, saying I had broken her heart. Physically really uncomfortable, want to get up, guts upset, hoping I will have to go to bathroom. Also thoughts of I will sit more today. Other not-so-strong thoughts of other things I will do today that need taking care of. Resolve to sit for the half hour I have specified. Go through a list of things to get done today. Open eyes and look around, look at time and sit for last ten minutes, calmer but still upset.

Meditating after an argument, a disappointment, a scare, or anything that throws us off balance can be very beneficial as a healing and learning process if we can develop the tolerance to be with the thoughts and feelings that are churned up. As you saw in this scenario, the meditator became calmer toward the end of the sitting by tolerating the intense feelings and not trying to manage or eliminate them. Like much of what I am pointing out in this book, the pattern is the opposite of what is often presented as correct meditation practice. His calmness follows upon a storm of feelings; it is not about creating a calm container to silence the storm.

Qualities are interlinked. Tolerance won't develop without other supporting qualities, which it in turn also supports. In the next two sections, I will focus on two other qualities that are cultivated by unlearning meditation: gentleness and interest.

Gentleness

I consider the quality of gentleness an important factor in unlearning meditation. It is primarily about being gentle with your harshness, irritation, anger, and impatience when those feelings are present. In this respect, it is intentional, as you remind yourself to be gentle with the pressured feelings, the self-critical voices, or the thoughts that demand your attention. After a while gentleness can start to arise in you without your having to remind yourself about it, and like many such qualities that we invoke or apply in meditation, it can then also emerge in situations where we least expect it, where it is most needed.

We all know what gentleness is like, even if we didn't experience much of it in our childhood or if we have had traumatic experiences that have eclipsed the softer side of humanity. It is being tender and caring when another is hurt or suffering. It is being friendly and understanding with someone. There is not only a soft voice but a soft demeanor, one that makes the gentle person also kind and trustworthy.

The qualities of self-acceptance, loving-kindness, and compassion all partake of this quality of gentleness, but those three qualities are more complicated, requiring learning, reminding, and practicing for most people, while gentleness is right there in front of us; it is at our fingertips, if we would only draw it out the rest of the way. That is what we are doing in unlearning meditation. We are clearing away what keeps us from being gentle with our own experience and that of others.

By not stopping our thoughts and feelings in meditation, we are paving the way for gentle ways of being with our experience. When thoughts are intentionally cut off, that is often an act of harming. If it is done aggressively, even with a minuscule amount of force, it supports and furthers the tendency to get rid of thoughts rather than the tendency to get to know them. Our ability to get to know our thoughts and feelings depends on our capacity to stay with them, and staying with them depends on our ability not to get rid of them. Holding our experience gently, thoughts and feelings come and go in their own time. What is cultivated is gentleness, not the feared obsession and domination by inner forces out of our control.

As you can see, gentleness is related to the qualities of tolerance and interest in your experience, the other two qualities talked about in this chapter. It links them emotionally. Investigation into your experience, when devoid of gentleness, can make you driven to find answers, get results, make conclusions and use them selfishly. Tolerance for pain, emotions, unwanted states of mind, and so forth can be practiced with a warrior mentality, where bearing pain to its limits is a mark of self-mastery. Tolerating what is painful with gentleness toward your reactions to the pain, and what the pain brings with it, feels more like embracing and comforting the pain than holding yourself rigidly in control of your reactions and feelings.

Interest in Your Experiences

As much as insight, understanding, wisdom, knowledge, and investigation into experience are talked about in relation to meditation practice, the simple quality that is at the root of all of these is seldom discussed. Teachers and traditions may differ in their opinions as to what that basic quality is, but I would hazard to propose that it is our interest in our experiences that enables us to become insightful, understanding, and wise regarding them. This of course goes against the notion that all you have to do is have an enlightening experience with the appropriate insights and all will be clear—that there is thus no need to waste your time looking at mundane or unacceptable experiences. I would say the opposite is actually true—by looking at our mundane and unacceptable experiences with an interested and open mind, insight, understanding, and investigation can actually be fostered.

Before you can really look at your mundane and unwanted experiences with interest, wonder, and curiosity, you may need to begin with your interest in the more compelling aspects of your meditation experience. I would not ask you to feign interest in things you have no interest in. It is more skillful to start with what you are naturally drawn to and then to work from there, as in this progression of meditation sittings from a woman who has meditated in this approach for a few years.

First Sitting: At one stage my attention went to my eyes . . . they were tight, as they usually are when I think. With my attention on them, they softened. My whole face softened. Sounds came from the window, and my attention leaped to the sound, as it wasn't obvious what it was. It was like I watched with interest as I saw the perception process kick in. It was a rumbling and a gravelly sound. I didn't put in effort. I just let it slowly register, and it took quite a few minutes.

Second Sitting: In the beginning of this sit there was a hodgepodge of various things that happened. But the whole way through as I was watching, or recollecting as I went along, there was a sort of theme in an overhanging question of "How do I know?" Something would occur, my mind would parcel it up into a story, but almost straightaway I would sort of challenge the experience, or at least challenge the label or view. I can't remember all of them, and its hard to frame now, but an example may be as follows. I would feel a tightness in my chest that I would watch for a while. I would think, "Chest tightness," but immediately there'd be this "maybe not" feel. I'd go into the tightness at another level and sense that maybe it was "joy." I'd think, "This is joy," but then up would come the, "maybe not" feel again. I'd sink into another layer of it and I'd think, "This is my energy thing," and I'd cut into another level of it and think, "This is a being-alive feeling." This would all happen in quite a short time, and it wasn't necessarily thought. But I'd just end up with the feeling/sensation, with no label or sense of what it was or who it was, just the sensation, then it would happen again. I remember feeling it as a layering process, and ending up with little sense of self, just the sensations that had gone through some natural kind of process of identity stripping.

The meditator was interested enough in how she was labeling her experiences to begin questioning the labels she was accustomed to using. Usually, meditators are instructed to investigate the nature of their sensations or the process of breathing, seeing them as arising and passing away or as having other general characteristics, but not to investigate the labels they use to describe experiences. With unlearning meditation, when you follow your interest, it goes to any aspect of your experience, not just a segment of it. Eventually a meditator will find that an interesting area of investigation has sparked an interest in related aspects, and so moves on to another area. Being interested is usually a dynamic quality, but we tend to try to hold our interests in check, as if there is some danger in pursuing new areas of curiosity that emerge. It is by allowing interests to expand and form in this way that interest starts to develop in aspects of our experience that have seemed bland or boring.

Here is a journal from another woman:

> Lots of thoughts about what I'm planning to do today. Roaming around. Then period of focused thoughts with interest—an idea for artwork. Followed the idea through for a while, developed it, visualized the piece.
>
> At some point thought came about breakfast—felt energy click in around the idea of what I wanted—quite subtle and quick, and then also very softly and quickly came a sort of turning away from that energy of wanting—just a turning away, maybe with a thought, something like "Oh, I don't have to go there right now." Subtle but distinct feeling of what it's like to renounce something, just leave it— an easing, opening.
>
> Then an impulse to go closer to that, at first wanting more of the easeful feeling, then feeling more interest in looking at the other side of the dynamic, at the feeling of restlessness under/inside the wanting. Was with that for a while—actually that's what I noticed first, rather than deciding to look at it.

At the beginning of the sitting, the meditator pursues visualizing an art project to its end, which, since she is an artist, is something that naturally grabs her interest. But when she moves on to thinking about breakfast, which is a comparatively mundane matter, her awareness of a subtle craving in the thoughts makes her interested. Her first response is to renounce the thoughts of wanting breakfast, and she experiences an opening around that. It feels easeful, and as much as she would want to have more of that feeling, what interests her is the other side of the experience: the restlessness inside/under the wanting.

The Subtle Nature of These Qualities

Tolerance, gentleness, and interest may be so subtle as to go largely unnoticed in meditation practice. These qualities may be more apparent at times when something that would normally be present, such as feeling pressured or using force, is absent. You may not realize that you were tolerating an intense emotion or an uncomfortable train of thought until after the sitting is over. In fact, you may not even give yourself much credit for tolerating something that in the past was difficult to tolerate, because in the act of tolerating it, you did very little. You probably just sat with the experience longer and with greater acceptance and patience.

Because many meditators are given the idea that good, wholesome qualities in meditation make themselves known to us by doing practices to generate them, there is less attention given to qualities that arise on their own. When gentleness arises of its own accord, with the conditions being right for it, it might appear more like a softening around your experience as opposed to some well-defined state of gentleness. You may just be soft and easy on yourself and not call it gentleness. In a similar way, you may suddenly find an old pattern of behavior emerge in a scenario within the meditation sitting, and instead of not wanting to go there, you'll be curious about it. You may not immediately consider that the quality of interest has arisen, but that doesn't matter—we don't need to identify these subtle qualities whenever they arise. We just need to acknowledge that such qualities are arising in our sittings from time to time and that cultivating them is allowing these qualities to lead and influence our meditation practice.

PART TWO

Impasses
and Calm Spaces

9

Impasses in Meditation

As I sit down to write this section on impasses, my thoughts also go to the two feet of snow that fell overnight outside my house. And there is more on the way today. In the interim, I must figure out how to get my car freed from the snow that surrounds it. Do I shovel it? For a shovel is all I have. Should I call someone to plow it for me? That involves starting a relationship with someone new, and before I do that, my wife will surely want to research it by talking to her friends and getting the word on the snowplow guys in town. Should I go over to my neighbor and ask to borrow his snowblower? That too has its complications. What if I just leave my car buried in the snow and wait until the snow melts? That might take weeks. During that time, I would have to rely on others to get food, mail, and supplies, and the garbage would begin to pile up in the house. Fortunately, we have enough food, firewood, and necessities stocked up to last a week or more, though we would need to take care of mail and trash. The question is: What do I do now with this impasse I am in?

I could simply decide not to concern myself with digging my car out of the snow and spend my time working on this book instead. It may be a blessing that I am snowed in at the moment, for I can concentrate on writing. But by not doing anything about it I am leaving the solution up to factors outside my volition, perhaps trusting that in time the conditions will change and I will be able to get my car out. This course of action requires patience, a willingness to make sacrifices, and a faith that things will turn out all right in the end.

Let's say this is also an acceptable way for working with impasses in meditation. Instead of doing something about the experience of being stuck, you put your attention on something you can do that is both beneficial and productive. Instead of paying attention to the sour mood or the angry thoughts you keep finding yourself in after a few minutes of sitting, you put your attention on your breath or on thoughts of loving-kindness or on a koan or mantra. You stay with something that is a productive use of your meditating time rather than attending to something that would seem to take up too much time and effort and require resources that you don't have. I could see how staying with a sour mood would be like my choosing to dig out my car with a snow shovel, while staying with a purposeful technique would be like my deciding to make the best use of my time by writing.

Still, even if I ignore the fact that I can't move my car, someday soon I will have to do something about it. Periodically during the day, mostly when I am taking a break from writing and am thinking of other things I need to do, I am reminded of the predicament with my car. It just doesn't go away because I am absorbed on something else. In fact, when the absorption fades, the predicament returns.

There is a fairly common belief that in meditation, if you stay with your breath, or in the present moment, or do any prescribed technique for long enough, you will have a transcendent experience, a realization, or some kind of internal shift in your way of being. This transformation is then supposed to eliminate the various negative moods and thoughts that keep you stuck doing and saying the same things over and over. Connected with this belief is the notion that impasses are overcome by such experiences and realizations without ever needing to be experienced fully and examined deeply. But as I said above, do you have the patience, can you make the sacrifices, and do you have the required faith to stay with a meditation practice that is supposed to overcome impasses by putting your attention on something other than the predicament your mind is in?

An impasse is "a predicament affording no obvious escape" according to *Webster's Third New International Dictionary*. Using that definition, one would find oneself at an impasse in meditation when there is no "obvious" way of going through something. All of the usual methods, the bright ideas and good advice, the right-sounding strategies and correct beliefs, don't help one go through something that one is stuck in, one's "predicament." There is a caged feeling around such impasses. You come face-to-face with your limitations, your ignorance, your lack of creativity, inventiveness, or insight.

It is easy to ignore such impasses when the purpose of meditation is taken to be doing the instruction correctly, trusting that doing so will eliminate all roadblocks and resolve all deadlocks. "What impasse?" you might ask. "My meditation practice is going just fine." Of course it is, on one level: the level where you have confidence and trust in your practice, believing in its effectiveness and correctness. But I wonder if on another level you feel stuck, confused, limited, or frustrated; if there are thoughts, feelings, and memories that keep repeating themselves as you sit; or if there are certain stories, themes, and problems that keep drawing you in and won't let go.

Working with an Impasse

Every meditation practice we do leads to an impasse. Often it is painfully obvious that what was working so well just the other day is no longer capable of delivering. The common advice meditation students get from teachers is to meditate harder. That is, to tighten around the instructions and put more time and effort into the practice. Sometimes a teacher will offer a strategy that he or she has used in a similar predicament. Occasionally the teacher might suggest that you take a break from meditation. This instruction misses the fact that tremendous learning can arise from staying with your impasses and exploring them more deeply.

Since I fully expect students to reach impasses, I am more than ready and willing to work with them on it. Some impasses are common for nearly everyone and can be addressed by the approach I have presented. Other impasses—the great majority of them—are highly individual. I can't just tell people what to do, because "doing something about it" in any form keeps them from tolerating the impasse and developing an interest in it. My approach here in this book is different and highly unorthodox.

Instead of giving you ways to work with or go through impasses, I am going to explore the impasses various students of mine have encountered. You may find that you relate to some of them in ways that illuminate aspects of your own impasses.

I would like to acknowledge that there is a tendency for teachers to present the successful and wonderful experiences students have had with their method. Sometimes that is the author's objective in writing the book—to show how well his method works. This does make a certain amount of sense when presenting a technique, but with a process of unlearning, there are periods that look like success, periods that look like failure, and periods that don't fit into either of those categories. By reading this book with an open and interested mind, you are engaged in the heart of my approach: exploration into the experience of meditating.

10

An Impassable Impasse

Cliff is a man in his fifties. He is primarily interested in Tibetan Buddhism and has been especially taken with the writings of Pema Chödrön. He came to me fairly content with his meditation practice, seeing no problem with it. After attending a one-day workshop in his hometown, he decided to keep a meditation journal and send it to me. Here is his account of what happened.

Day one: Started with tracking breathing sensations in abdomen or heart areas. Sitting began without apparent difficulty other than trying to be comfortable. Thought about how to do it right. Had a fair amount of anxiety about doing meditation correctly and tried to just follow thoughts and feelings associated with fear of doing meditation wrong. Felt some anxiety but stayed present. Tried to be aware of the person doing the thinking and follow that inward. Noticed my left leg falling asleep. Felt tremendous fear of doing it wrong. Was again present with fear. Aware of constant thinking. Session ended and seemed to pass quickly.

From this account, it seems Cliff's most prominent impasse is his fear of doing meditation wrong. This arose after an apparently smooth beginning of tracking breathing sensations in his chest. What was the practice he thought he had to do right, and feared doing wrong? Was it watching his breath? Or was it allowing his thoughts and feelings into the meditation and becoming aware of them?

Day two: Sat with some difficulty getting a comfortable position for my legs. Transition seemed smooth. I went to noticing sensations of breathing at the abdomen and heart. Dwelt on doing meditation correctly. Tended to notice I was thinking and then as soon as I became aware of thinking, the thought would dissolve, or I would notice my thinking and then become aware of "who" was doing the noticing. Would try to be gentle with this "technique" and notice how good it felt to be kind and avoid judgments; felt rather warm and a little exhilarated. Began thinking I was doing meditation wrong and felt a little low and then noticed the thinking. . . . As meditation wore on, I became more engrossed in thoughts for longer periods before I became aware I was thinking. Thoughts of doing the meditation wrong came up repeatedly, and I felt bad about that. Then I felt some confusion, but each time that feeling of confusion came I would let the feeling be there with equanimity until the feeling lifted. Had a few thoughts wondering when meditation would be over but resisted looking at the timer. Meditation seemed to go quickly and ended sooner than expected. Felt like time was brief in general. I just allowed thoughts and feelings to arise naturally and attempted to meet each with gentleness, allowing whatever thought or feeling to arise and run its course. . . . My state at the end was about the same as at the start.

I get the sense from this entry that Cliff is using three different techniques in his sitting. One is awareness of the breath as sensations around his abdomen and chest. It is a practice he dwells on doing correctly. The second is a way of noticing who is doing the noticing, which is a practice of trying to be aware of awareness or knowing knowing. The third practice he uses is stated at the end: allowing thoughts and feelings to arise naturally and run their course—essentially the instruction I gave him. Each of these three practices has its own rules, concepts, values, and beliefs, and though it may seem like they can be integrated into one practice by putting them into a sequence or using them as strategies, in actual practice they contradict each other. Awareness of breathing comes with a different set of rules than allowing thoughts and feelings does. Noticing the observer of one's experience requires the concentration that would otherwise be put on the breath, and such concentration would not be conducive to a more open and receptive way of being in meditation. No wonder Cliff encountered confusion. But instead of seeing how the confusion was an important aspect of his impasse, he treated it as something to pacify and get beyond.

> Day three: I began meditation sitting in cross-legged position after lighting a candle. By the end of the meditation, my legs are usually asleep, but that happened with less intensity today. Worried today that I wasn't spending time with awareness of bodily sensations, i.e., feelings in legs, abdomen, and chest. Thought about a conversation I had with a buddy over dinner and then noticed the thinking, and then the thoughts seemed to dissolve. Then thought about a conversation with a woman I am meeting for the first time (for dating). When I think about stuff like this without being aware that I am thinking, I judge myself for not noticing. Then I try to be gentle and then I feel afraid for being too gentle, like I will lose myself if I am not judging. A few times I became briefly restless, but the feeling of restlessness passed. I did not pay much attention to my breathing for the rest of the time. Meditation seemed to pass quickly and ended smoothly. I was surprised how

quickly the time went by. Felt slightly disappointed that I did not have some kind of profound experience.

Cliff's description of this sitting hints at a subtle shift in his practice. He doesn't pay much attention to his breathing and lets himself think about things without noticing that he is thinking about them. He knows he has broken some rule about being aware of each thought, for that also seems to be a practice he has done. He judges himself for it. When he is then gentle with himself, he feels he will lose himself if he is not judging. Could his impasse also have an aspect to it of being afraid of losing a part of himself that judges?

> Day five (skipping over day four): Began sitting with feelings of frustration because I don't know how to do this meditation. Began noticing chest and abdominal breathing. Kept thinking about frustration again. Judged myself for thinking again. Then remembering to be gentle and accepting of thinking. Then beat myself up for forgetting to be gentle. Noticed I was gentle on myself and then became afraid I was doing it wrong. Very scary to not think or to allow myself to think gently. Feel more comfortable judging. When I judge, I know who I am. I kept going back to noticing who was thinking, which launches me into new streams of thinking. Noticed again how scary it is to be gentle with myself. When I think, I am afraid that in the gentleness I lose myself. Even writing this I feel frustration. I am not doing this right. Had many thoughts about what to remember to write when the meditation ended. Overriding thought is that when I judge myself for thinking, I know who I am. When I am gentle on me, I feel scared because I don't know who I am. The lack of judgment feels ungrounded, like it "can't be right." I'm not really aware of a transition period. I just try to be gentle. The focus of thoughts is about being gentle. I still am averse to thinking even when I am trying to be gentle. Did not

pay more attention to breathing because I decided that was not what I was supposed to be doing during meditation. I am supposed to notice thoughts. Paying attention to chest and abdominal breathing feels too easy and peaceful. I sort of decided I need to stay with noticing thoughts, which is more difficult and takes work. Meditation ended with left leg aching because it fell asleep. I was ready to have meditation end.

In this sitting Cliff is more actively "doing" my approach to meditation, holding on to the instruction to be gentle with his experience. It has the unanticipated effect of producing fear and a loss of self. But it is also showing him that he is strongly identified with judging. The impasse comes into clearer focus: the meditator self is also a judging self. He is afraid to be gentle, to be open and allowing. He is identified with that part of himself that is harsh, critical, and judgmental.

Just consider that predicament for a little while. I am sure it is a familiar one for some of you. Those of you who have been caught in this impasse probably have not found an "obvious" escape.

Any meditation instruction that is taken up, even for a few minutes, will probably have some harshness in it. Trying to be gentle would probably be done harshly, with force. Trying to do any meditation practice will set Cliff up for failure, for even if he does it well for a while, there will be times when he can't do it all that well. If he is told a particular strategy to apply, it will turn into something that will be judged. In short, there is nothing for him to do, for by doing anything, he is stepping into a situation where he will judge himself.

Does this sound like an impasse to you? It does to me. If I were Cliff's teacher, which I was at the time of this journal, I would have to pause and reflect on the overall situation. So I am pausing now to reflect a moment. As I do, I am reminded of something a longtime student once said about her experiences of judging. Her judgments were like snapping turtles. Each time she thought about a particular person or a certain situation, the attitude underneath the judging looked like snapping turtles. It seemed so automatic to her. A memory would appear, a snap judgment would follow. She continued to sit thinking and snapping at the people in her thoughts. She would even catch herself snapping at herself on occasion. How did this clear up for her? She just kept observing this process repeat itself and started to find it interesting. Once she really understood how judging worked, she was able to unlearn it. Not completely, but enough for it not to be such a big impasse anymore.

Just knowing how something operates in the moment may not be enough to dislodge the impasse. It is a common view in meditation circles that you don't need to know the history of something that arises—all you need to do is be with the present-moment experience of it. What I see is that we need to know both: the present manifestation and the past memory.

Exploring the past often feels too psychological for many students. That is, it seems to be a way to build more stories and feed more beliefs around the experience. Take judging, for example. Your personal history of it would have to include your parents, your teachers, friends, and enemies. It would have to include traumatic experiences of being judged and punished, as well as chronic situations where you felt inferior and under the watchful gaze of a judging authority figure. You might reexperience dimly remembered episodes of being shamed, of being rejected, of being teased, and of not getting it right. This exposure to your past would be uncomfortable, and it might bring to the surface pain that you don't have the time or inclination to deal with right now. That is all right. You don't need to push yourself to go there.

Still, the past can be explored as it comes up naturally. To do this you need to let random memories come into the sitting and hold off making sense out of them or interpreting them. Instead, let yourself reexperience the past events, or the feelings that come up with those memories, and do nothing with them. The memories may not fit into the theme or issues you are looking at, so you don't need to try to force a fit. After a while of sitting with memories, they will dissipate, disappear, or open up into an area to explore, as in this meditation sitting a student sent me recently.

I had an interesting sit last night. As you know, I have been struggling with the pain of loneliness for months, since I moved away from my wife and children on account of work. Last night, in a lengthy sit (of about two hours), I was face-to-face with my feelings of loneliness with an unprecedented degree of clarity. I experienced a series of hurtful memories and imagined scenarios involving suffering due to separation from my loved ones. Some memories were recent, others from my teens, and yet others from my early childhood. Almost all the memories and fantasies were about the same theme—not being able to "have" my loved ones. I had thoughts related to my parents, close relatives, friends, ex-lovers, my partner, and my children. Some of the most compelling memories/fantasies were with respect to an ex-lover, who despite a very strong, passionate connection between us in the past, chose not to live with me and rejected my marriage proposal. In last night's sit, I again felt rejected, abandoned, insulted, alone, angry, jealous of another person who "has" my lover who I should have "had." As with almost all sits, this sit was not all linear or cleanly laid out in coherent stories. Rather, it was more like short stories—configurations of thoughts, memories, imagined future scenarios mixed with anger at times, hurt at other times. These stories would come and go. There were periods of calm, and then another story would rise again. Sometimes I had work-related thoughts, but they were sparse. Sometimes I would be deeply absorbed in a dynamic interior space. But the sit was mostly about stories related to not "having" my loved ones. What's striking is that while all of the drama was going on, I understood that all of these seemingly compelling stories were merely reflections or constructions of my own mind. I had a whole new point of view from which I saw this current of hurtful experiences flowing together, coloring each other, incorporating or reconstructing memories since my childhood. Until last night, there had been a lingering undercurrent of something that I had been labeling as "loneliness." This was no longer present. I ended the sit after the stories completely subsided and went to bed. I slept like a baby afterward. When I woke up this morning, the unrest of "loneliness" was not there, as it is most mornings.

11

A Partially Cleared Impasse

Yesterday evening, a friend of ours plowed the snow behind our Toyota 4Runner. Unfortunately, we didn't know about it until this evening, when it was too late to dig out the remainder of the car. Besides, it had begun to snow again. Our friend had anticipated that we would go up to the car and see that the snow had been plowed. When our dog was alive, we would take daily walks, even in heavy snow, as he loved the snow. But since he passed away, we have been taking fewer walks and try not to walk much outdoors after the snow has frozen, for it is too slippery. I had thought of going up to the car around noon when I was outside collecting firewood, because I noticed a small John Deere used for snowplowing at a neighbor's house and had thought of asking the person to plow my driveway, but then I decided not to. If I had, I would have discovered that the berm behind our car had been leveled flat, though the car's tires were still buried in snow and ice. But then I would have spent a couple of hours digging snow and would not have written parts of the previous chapter. In fact, I was so absorbed in writing that for the most part, I had no thoughts of going into town and getting supplies or driving to the dump or meeting a friend for tea.

By not doing anything and being unaware of the current state of the predicament causing an ongoing impasse, the predicament improved, almost to the point of being resolved. But not quite. It still required my attention to fully resolve it. And it took someone else to act on it in order for it to improve.

Let me take this metaphor and apply it to a way of working with impasses in meditation. Being absorbed in something, like the breath, and ignoring the current state of some kind of predicament one has experienced before in meditation can work on an impasse to a degree but, in my opinion, not completely. When I referred to the belief of ignoring an impasse and just trusting your method of meditation to eliminate it, I was not referring to this situation. This is different. Here, you go in and out of the impasse. When you are free of it for a while, you still know that the predicament will reappear and reassert itself at some point down the line. At that point you need to be willing to look at it. And it may truly be diminished and thus easier to tolerate.

There is a definite interplay between impasses and calm spaces. In these instances, the impasse may manifest as a type of impediment or hindrance, such as are described in the Buddhist literature. As a hindrance, it is an obstacle to becoming calm and focused. Generally, calmness and a sense of well-being are what meditators are seeking. They are not usually seeking to know more about what gets in the way of being calm, but would rather know how to get through hindrances and arrive at calm states of mind. Primarily for that reason, such hindrances are not deemed worthy of investigation, and so meditators are often not interested in them. And yet, a hindrance such as restlessness (worries, anxieties, fears) may take up much of a sitting.

What makes a hindrance an impasse, in my opinion, is when it recurs in an oppressive and constricting way. So that even when you pass through a period of being lustful or hateful to a period of settled mind, the lust and the hate return sometime after the calm state has passed. When you find yourself cycling back and forth between calmness and chaos, then you may notice that what you have taken as a temporary hindrance is actually "a predicament affording no obvious escape."

I could draw from countless reports on meditation sittings from students to support what I am saying, but to illustrate it for you, I will use the first journal I received from a student whom I have now worked with for nearly five years.

His name is Jonathan. His meditation practice began with some classes in Mindfulness Based Stress Reduction, in which he primarily learned to focus on the breath at the abdomen. He went on to attend a couple of ten-day Goenka Vipassana meditation retreats and then some retreats led by an American Vipassana teacher. On retreat he would do the meditation practice he was taught, and he saw himself as a willing and obedient student who needed some kind of formalized, structured technique in order to meditate. After the retreats, he would generally revert back to his initial meditation practice of just observing the breath, remaining, however, still very much concerned about doing it right.

When he first contacted me, I suggested he keep a journal for a week and send it to me. Here is what he wrote.

Day one (40 min.): Felt less agitated than in previous sits. Wondering, "What should I be doing?" . . . "What should I be noting for later recollections?" . . . Then lost in images, many of which I don't remember. But when I became aware of the fact that I had gone off somewhere, there was a feeling of alarm, which had a punitive feel to it (like I had messed up and been caught by someone [i.e., me]). It was at that point that I would intentionally become aware of the still points of contact. Then more thoughts, "Am I doing this correctly?" Noticed that my mind was generally open to the sounds outside, feeling of being able to hold sounds and bodily sensations in awareness. Thoughts seemed like free association in image form. No clear awareness of feelings/emotions that went with it.

As you can see from this journal entry, Jonathan needed more guidance than the initial instructions I gave him, which are the same instructions I gave in chapter 2. Even if he received instructions from me that said "Just do this and nothing else," he would end up wondering if he was doing those instructions correctly. His meditation practice is filled with this impasse around instructions: when given little or no structure, he is concerned about what he should be doing; when given structure, he is concerned about whether he is doing the instruction correctly.

He is also meditating with the rule not to let his mind wander. This rule operates as an impediment for him to see and know the impasse he is in. This is a bit complex to explain, but please try to follow my thinking on this. First of all, it is impossible to meditate without your mind leaving the object(s) of meditation for periods of time. Your mind will wander often in meditation, and you will have trains of thought that are unusual, unwanted, and unsatisfying, as well as thoughts that are familiar, acceptable, and compelling. You really don't have much control over what you will think, but you do have more control over how you react to the thinking and what you then decide to do about it. So, in a meditation practice where thinking is disallowed, the act of stopping your thoughts is also an act of controlling your experience. The rule about not allowing thinking to progress in meditation is just a rationalization for various acts of suppressing, controlling, and denying of thoughts. By trying to control his experience, Jonathan gets caught in the bind of wondering what he should do or whether he is doing the technique correctly. The way out of the bind is to sit with less control. That alone will reduce the tension between instructions and the mind as it is.

Day two (50 min.): Mind almost immediately goes to scenarios at work. Being in a meeting, speaking in the meeting, and in some way, impressing people. A sense of self-aggrandizing. Then, upon noticing this, an awareness of feeling very deflated, sad, small. Came back to still points of contact. Level of agitation and restlessness increased.

Mind goes to scenario of TV show *Six Feet Under.* When I'd notice I was thinking about the show there would be fear. Came back to feelings of hands on legs and noticed high levels of agitation in the body. A feeling of wanting to jump out of my skin. Mind jumped quickly from thing to thing but calmer in a way as it was jumping. Less aware of agitation when I allowed my mind to do that. A few times my mind settled on the gentle up-and-down movement of my diaphragm but could not stay with it for long. Dropped off for some time, then an awareness of having thoughts that were scary, upsetting. Not the thoughts themselves, but the realization that I had had those thoughts. More anxiety in the body, then self-talk, "Why am I having these thoughts?" "What does this mean?" Feelings of anxiety at "not having an anchor" in the meditation. Also an awareness of music (Dylan) in the background of my mind.

In this sitting we can see an obvious reason why Jonathan doesn't sit with less control. It makes him agitated and anxious not to have an anchor (not to keep returning to the breath). He lets his mind wander to several things in the meditation: a situation at work, a TV show, a song, feelings he was having. He remarks that he felt less agitated, calmer, when he let his mind jump from thing to thing. But the process of allowing his mind such freedom in meditation also exposed him to thoughts that he was scared to think, and yet these thoughts came to him unbidden. Being receptive and allowing of your mind in meditation can lead to calmness as well as agitation, and permits what was disavowed in your prior meditation practice to rise to the surface.

Notice that somewhere in the middle of the sitting he dropped off for some time. I would need much more description to say more about it than it was another way he lost control, but this time in a pleasant and relaxing way—though he may not acknowledge that, because he "dropped off," thus associating the experience with sleep, and we all know that falling asleep in meditation is breaking a fairly common rule.

Day three (45 min.): Almost immediately aware of places of stillness (legs on the ground, hands on my thighs). Mind less chaotic, not jumping so quickly. The mind seemed able to land on one scenario and stay there for a longer period. During the sit my mind came back to stillness quite frequently and was able to recall where it had been, but I am unable to do that right now as I try to recall it to write it down. Mostly thoughts involved day-to-day occurrences, but there would be moments where fear would come on the tails of an unwanted thought. During much of the sit, I felt split between deep stillness and activity (concurrently), even with moments of agitation (vibrating in the body). I was watching it from a place that was very calm. I remember moments that involved thoughts, "I could do this for a long time." Almost a sense of deep relaxation inside the agitation/vibration. My awareness moved to my breath for a short period. A feeling of being okay while taking everything in (sounds from upstairs, going in and out of thinking). Mind became more foggy toward the end. Went into thought where I was gone for longer periods of time, but seemed less judgmental (of myself) when I came back from dropping off.

This meditation began with greater stillness and ease than the prior ones. There appears to be no need for Jonathan to control his experience in this sitting. He lets his mind stay with a scenario for as long as it lasts, finding that being with thoughts and feelings can go on concurrently with a sense of stillness. His awareness moved to breath for a period of time, but he did not intentionally move it there. The breath was like everything else he was taking in or landing on for a while. Even at the end of the sit, "dropping off" had much less judgment attached to it.

Day four (50 min.): Aware of sound almost constantly in my mind. Songs in my head seemed more prominent than usual (Randy Newman songs). Mind went to different scenarios regarding my children. Lost in thoughts for a long time, but part of me seemed to be aware of the fact that I was thinking. When I'd notice that I was, I would come back to my contact points in a more matter-of-fact way. There was little, if any, judgment directed toward myself for having been thinking. At one point I became aware of my breath, followed by confusion, "Should I be focusing on my breath? By doing that am I following the instruction? What the hell should I be doing?" etc. . . . . More agitation in the body. Looked at the clock a few times. Suddenly aware of feeling very calm. Surprised by this.

The impasse returned in this sitting, even though Jonathan had less judgment about thinking. He was meditating with less force, coming back to his contact points (i.e., hands touching) in a more relaxed way. But when he found his attention on the breath, the confusion started, and with it the impasse reappeared, accompanied by bodily agitation. Upon reading this, I ask myself, "Why is he unable to be aware of the thoughts about what he should be doing in the same way he is aware of other thoughts?" In other words, "What is the hook in the thoughts about what he should be doing?"

There is obviously much more to this impasse than needing to control his experience. From discussing it with him, it seems that it has something to do with needing an authority figure. He can't be the one who decides what he should be doing or determines that he is doing it right. He needs someone to do that for him. When he asks the question, "By doing this [following the breath] am I following the instruction [Jason gave me]?" he is expressing a need to have me tell him that following the breath "is" or "is not" the instruction I gave him. He needs me to be definite about that, and I can't. When awareness of the breath enters into his experience, that is what he is experiencing, and I would encourage him to be with it. He is not making himself aware of the breath in any forceful way or trying to be aware only of the breath. And if he were practicing breath meditation in a forceful way, I would ask him to become aware of that, not to stop it.

I am a confusing teacher for some people. I admit it. Sometimes the way the teacher teaches is a contributing factor to a meditator's impasse. In this case, I believe the way I teach can actually bring this side of the impasse into view. For if I were a teacher who taught formal, structured meditation practices, then Jonathan would be preoccupied with doing my instructions correctly. But since I am teaching an open, flexible, minimally structured approach to meditation, he has the added discomfort of being confused as to what the instructions are. This presents him with an authority figure who is not giving him anything specific to do. This is unfamiliar and unsettling. So he occasionally has to see me as the kind of teacher who gives instructions that students either succeed or fail at. I can accept that projection. It is perfectly natural for the role I am in. Still, I have to remind him, and other students in this predicament, that there is no wrong experience when doing Recollective Awareness Meditation.

> Day five (35 min.): Initially mind focused on points of stillness. A feeling of pleasure at just staying with the stillness (not thinking as much about whether I am doing it right, what I should be noticing for my journal, etc.). Noticed my mind would move into fantasy: one involved standing at the top of my street, seeing a bunch of green grapes rolling down it. Aware that I am unable to stop the grapes from rolling away. An out-of-control feeling. This was very much like a dream state. Noticed that fear or "being caught" (surprised) seemed to precipitate my mind's leaving the still points of contact. Also aware of my awareness being split concurrently (felt like layers of awareness) between still points of contact, vibrations in the body, fear, as well as quick activity in the visual field (all at the same time). My mind then moved into analysis, trying to ascertain if it is fear or something else I am experiencing. Noticed that agitation in my body increased as I tried to figure this out.

It was at this point that I opened my eyes, looked around, looked at the clock. The rest of the sit was very anxious in the body. A subtle shakiness in most of my body. Thoughts, "Maybe this is the coffee I drank." Through most of this though I felt pleased at having a vantage point in the stillness to observe my experience.

In this sitting, the impasse once more disappears, and Jonathan is conscious of its absence. It is not gone for good, as it pops its head up every so often in his journals over the next couple of years. It comes and goes but is still strongly rooted, for his need for structure and certainty in his meditation practice has deeper and far more extensive roots than he knows.

12

Getting Through an Impasse

Today is a beautiful sunny day, a bit warmer than yesterday, with about two inches of freshly fallen snow on the ground and in the trees. As the sun heats up, clumps of snow fall from the trees. The snow on the ground and around our car is softer and easier to shovel, though more dense and therefore heavier. My wife and I are going to try to get the car dug out. We'll use the tools we have at our disposal and our past knowledge of what we've done in similar situations, and with determination to see it to the end, we will hopefully be driving into town this afternoon. If we fail—which is entirely possible—we'll have to wait until after the next storm, which is scheduled to arrive this evening, to pass. It's reported to be a big one, and we may end up with another foot of snow to clear.

We concentrate our efforts around the tires. The big, flat-edged snow shovels are too clumsy to maneuver around the tires, so my wife gathers some gardening tools: a small hand shovel, a couple of small trowels, and a stick to poke through the snow and loosen it. So, even though there are piles of snow all around the car, we get down on our knees and carefully dig out the tires. Falling snow from the tree branches above fills in some of the spaces as we dig, so we remove larger clumps of snow with a shovel as we go. It gets easier, because the snow below the top frozen layer is soft, fluffy, and light. It takes us about an hour to get the car cleared enough to start her up and drive out into the street.

Impasses in meditation are usually bigger, heavier, and more difficult to manage than we think. Awareness can help us whittle them down, become more tolerant of them, and explore them. We can even concurrently develop enough tranquillity to make the impasse temporarily subside. This process requires patience and perseverance. At some point, meditation with the impasse becomes more fruitful and less frustrating, and you can begin to see a light at the end of the tunnel. That's when the time is ripe to dig in and get to the roots of the impasse.

This is delicate work, requiring a skilled and gentle touch. Bear in mind, though, that there are no universal instructions, no proven strategies that work for everyone.

Impasses
HEAVY AND LIGHT

Most impasses start heavy, and as you progress in unlearning meditation, they tend to become lighter and easier to be with and go through. That's because the habits you're unlearning are what have made an impasse heavy or difficult to begin with. With those habits unlearned for the most part, creative and intuitive ways of being with the impasse can emerge.

A heavy impasse becomes lighter as soon as you "loosen" around the meditation instructions and allow yourself more flexibility. As the impasse becomes less weighty, you may be able to question the views and beliefs of a particular practice and not just drop it because it doesn't work, but also loosen your grip around the notion of the correctness or rightness of that practice. As the impasse gets even lighter, you might even find that the practice that wasn't working for you arises in a different way and that you're able to do it for a little while, experience its benefits, and let go of it. At that point the impasse is no longer operating, and instead of feeling like you have made some great breakthrough, you just might feel a little lighter, as if a load had been taken off your shoulders. Meditation is really as easy and pleasant as you had hoped.

Many impasses are made up of concepts and the mental constructs built up around them, and those are harder to become aware of than the ones that just pertain to meditation practice. The constructs may have to do with beliefs about reality, about the nature of existence, the truth of things, and so forth. They may also be personal narratives about your life or the people in it. They may also be reasons, justifications, and explanations for various behaviors and attitudes that have been running your life from behind the scenes. It's an interesting area to explore, and it's one toward which unlearning meditation inevitably will take you.

Transformative Conceptualization

Transformative conceptualization is what I call the framework I have developed for looking into the mental constructs that support an impasse. It is a way of examining what we have come to know and believe to be true about certain kinds of experience. The things we hold to be true about ourselves, others, and the world can keep us in a light impasse for a long time.

One of the major beliefs that must be questioned before a transformative conceptualization process can work is the belief that nonconceptual understanding comes from "pure" sense experience. With that belief unexamined, you will not be open to this process, which, in fact, states the opposite: the nonconceptual is arrived at through awareness, discernment, and investigation into your own experience. There is a common belief that the Buddha was teaching people to become aware of the senses in a way that led to only pure sense experience for one who attained liberation. Some people extend this notion to include the preverbal stage of infancy and think that a liberated mind would be like an infant's mind, having no concepts. But we cannot go backward to a world of no concepts once we have progressed along the line of using concepts. I believe the Buddha was actually teaching a development of mind through a refining and clarifying of the conceptualizing process to the point where, free from concepts, one is also free from beliefs concepts create. To get there, however, you need to travel the path of investigating your beliefs, views, and models of experience. Here we have another aspect of unlearning meditation.

So how does this transformative conceptualization process work? It works in three basic steps.

1. Naming an experience
2. Describing that named experience
3. Seeing into the narrative of that experience

Naming the Experience

The first step in conceptualizing our experience happens when we give it a name. There are two ways we generally do this. The first way is to learn a concept beforehand and then look for it in our experience. "Doubt" would be one such concept. When we then have an experience that matches doubt as we've conceived it, we designate that experience "doubt."

The other way we tend to conceptualize our experiences with names is when we have an experience and then name it while it is happening (or sometime afterward). For example, you're sitting in meditation and you're so frustrated with the meditation instructions that you conclude this sort of meditation isn't for you. At the time, the experience may not be named, but on reflection, you might end up calling the experience doubt.

Normally you would stop there at this first step of conceptualization, especially if your teacher or your peers accept that word as the correct label for that experience. The word *doubt* may actually be part of the vocabulary of the meditation teaching you've received, just as its opposite, the word *faith,* may also be. If you conceptualize doubt, you may identify yourself or be identified by others in the community as a doubter. Such conceptualization quite readily lends itself to labeling and to personal identification with the label.

Describing the Named Experience

The second step of this conceptualization process comes when you begin to describe the named experience in more detail. In doing that you might find out several things about the experiences that escape notice when a name is used for them. For instance, you might describe how you try to do the instruction to the best of your ability and yet are periodically pulled away by thoughts and feelings. Or, in unlearning meditation, you will likely experience periods of confusion about what you're supposed to be doing in the sitting. You might also wonder if this approach is aimless or counterproductive. By describing what you call doubt in more detail, you can become aware of how you have been using doubt to name a variety of different experiences that may share some qualities, but are not exactly the same.

You may also notice that when you describe your experiences, there can be confusion about the language you have chosen to describe them, especially if the words come from a system of thought, such as Buddhist teachings—that is, if the words you're using to describe your experiences aren't your own. You might find that when you begin to use your own words, the experience starts to sound different. For example, you call one sort of experience of doubt "being confused about what to do," and another "not being convinced of the validity of this teaching."

By describing experiences in greater depth and detail, you might discover things about them that you missed on earlier passes. There is more going on than meets the eye—not all of our experience makes it into language when we use a single word to describe it. What gets put into that single word is a selected area of experience that fits it, but not the aspects of the experience that don't.

Many times we bypass the step of naming and go to describing instead. When we can't find the right word for some emotion and launch into a lengthy description of the experience instead, that is what we are doing. We are conceptualizing with a description rather than just a single word. But we often go through such descriptions in order to find a single word for the experience, as if every experience has a name if we can only find out what it is. In this process of transformative conceptualization, you can come up empty-handed and let the description, the story, the poem, or the picture be what represents the experience for you.

In calling back to mind a meditation sitting, you might verbalize segments of experience or visualize them, using descriptions. You might also use single words to describe experiences, though the word may be only a place marker for the greater and more nuanced awareness of the experience. General characteristics of one's experiences may come back, such as the texture of a state of mind, the tone of a narrative voice, the sense of space or place, or the underlying mood that pervaded the sitting. The bits and pieces of the meditation sitting, the highs and lows of it, the qualities that were present and those that were absent, are just some of things that will enter into the description. The description of a sitting can be of anything that occurred in it, and yet it does not have to be totally complete.

There are many elements of your sittings that won't make it into words, pictures, or impressions, but these may be remembered still. It is nearly impossible to represent them to yourself completely, much less convey them to another. But they are still part of your description.

The description and the experience it describes are joined together, just like when you use the name for an experience to describe it when you talk about it. When you describe, for example, "a confusion over what I should be doing in meditation," that description can be applied to other similar experiences and may even be used when you're having such an experience as the way of noticing it. Or you might note such experiences with the shorthand, single-word description "confusion."

A transformative conceptualization process has developed here. The name for an experience now comes from a description of it, and both name and description are used when talking about it. The conceptualizing may then go further, where new, more honest descriptions form out of being with such experiences, and consequently, the name used to designate the experience may come into question and be found lacking, whereby a new name (or description) will be sought. As the process continues, naming may become very difficult, and describing may become the only viable way of conceptualizing your experiences.

Seeing into the Narrative of an Experience

Seeing into the narrative of an impasse usually takes a certain amount of experiential familiarity with it over time, as well as a lightening of the impasse through the initial two steps of the transformative conceptualization process. It can still be done when the impasse is somewhat heavy, but not when it is impassable, for in such a case you would most likely encounter frustration. There needs to be some period of time in which you are not completely embedded in the impasse in order for you to see into it in the ways I am about to describe.

In addition to impasses around concepts like doubt, we also have our own personal narratives about having faith in something or someone, or the opposite—distrusting people, authorities, religions, and so forth. Our own history with the religion we were brought up in might arise. We may remember how we were treated in it, what we learned in it, and the views and morality it gave us that still influence us. Or if not a religion, then maybe a memory—of a club, a team, an organization, an institution, or any situation where one had to "believe" in a program or a person— may appear as supporting or feeding this experience of doubt. It may be that rebelling against authority figures is something you do quite reflexively, while other people quite naturally trust someone who is an authority. Or you might find your personal narratives to be somewhere between these extremes: you're cautious about what you believe in, needing to ask questions and test things out over time, or you're only willing to trust someone after having observed his or her motives and character on a number of occasions.

Our narratives around teachings play a large part in keeping the impasse of doubt alive, and they may be harder to detect and investigate than the personal narratives we are more familiar with. We may be living with a rather simple narrative that we should believe everything about the teachings we are practicing and not question them, since they come from someone wiser and more spiritually developed than we are. But that view leads to dependence on the teacher, or his or her tradition, and does not usually allow us to have critical thoughts about the practices we're doing and the teachings we're receiving. The belief that we should not doubt our teacher (which is strong in many Buddhist traditions) turns the experience of doubt into an area of conflict, bringing up the fear of being rejected by the teacher and having to find another. If only more teachers of meditation could accept the role doubt, confusion, and critical thinking play in a meditator's development of independence and autonomy, they could perhaps support it as something healthy for the individual instead of seeing it as a rejection of their teachings or betrayal of their trust.

Conflict with the narratives often arises within this process, and this process of conflict is essential for anyone who wants to fully examine the concepts he or she has taken on in meditation practice. When we start to withdraw our belief in the various narratives that are sustaining impasses, it is not just a simple rejection of those narratives; rather, it is facing the import and significance that those narratives have had for our practice. You can still respect and value the teachers and the teachings they've imparted to you while at the same time believing in them less and less and seeing into them more and more. Perhaps the main reason many people resist the path of unlearning meditation has to do with not knowing how to question a teaching, or a teacher's method, without rejecting it. It's likely that some elements of your meditation practice will be dropped in the process, as will certain concepts, but the invaluable and irreplaceable elements will still remain a part of your continuing practice.

In this process of transformative conceptualization, new narratives will be generated in your meditation practice, ones based on the new descriptions and the new ways of seeing things. These new narratives may help you through impasses. Such narratives, and there can be many that will come to you, function for the time when they are fresh and vital, but often lose their ability to affect experience as they become stale and turn into concepts divorced from the experiences they arose alongside.

An Initial Transformative Conceptualization

Toward the end of my time as a Buddhist monk in Sri Lanka, I went through this transformative conceptualizing process after unlearning meditation. After I had unlearned much of the practice taught by Mahasi Sayadaw of noting each moment of my experience, I began to study particular discourses of the Buddha's that listed the various elements of our mental world. I combined this study with further reading in the Abhidhamma, notably the book mentioned in an earlier chapter, *A Comprehensive Manual of Abhidhamma*. The model I was then using to understand my meditative experience was one heavily based on naming each experience and having that name relate to something that truly exists as found in these texts.

With the belief that craving exists with a pleasant sensation, I would notice pleasant sensations and see the craving that arose with them. With the belief that anger arose with unpleasant sensations, I would notice unpleasant sensations with that association in mind. By doing so, I believed I was seeing the truth of craving and anger (or aversion), and by naming my experiences as such, I was getting at the core reality of those experiences. Along with naming these experiences, I was seeing them as arising and passing away, even when they seemed to last for some time, as I had developed the habit of breaking down all of my experiences into successive moments of discrete, separate events. I became an avid observer who tried to notice every moment as it arose and passed away, making each fit a name that was connected with a system of names found either in the Buddha's discourses or in the later Abhidhamma.

I found myself engaged in this practice of naming my experiences mostly when I was doing walking meditation or at other times outside of a meditation sitting. When I sat, I would mostly name experiences that were either defilements or hindrances, and sometimes I would name subtler or more wholesome states of mind, though I mostly left those unnamed. I was more interested in the subtle wholesome states of mind and so tended to reflect on them more, explore them in greater depth, and come up with descriptions for them. The unwholesome states of mind were less interesting, and in accordance with the meditation culture in which I found myself, my aim was to overcome, diminish, or transcend them. Naming them as they arose was the accepted way of working with them.

After some months of meditating like this, it occurred to me to make a distinction between hindrances and unwholesome mental states. The sense-desire found in a hindrance was essentially the same as the "mind state with craving accompanied by a pleasant sensation" except for one significant difference: The hindrance of desire persisted for a longer period of time and made it difficult to get settled and focused. The mind state of desire could be far shorter, even lasting only a few seconds, and did not hinder my mind from getting settled and focused. I was not as engrossed or embedded in transitory mind states, as they could even occur while I was calm and concentrated but not affect the peace and calm I was experiencing. While, on the other hand, a hindrance would have me in its grip for a while, and I would have to go through it before my mind would settle.

When I applied this conceptualization to another experience that arose in meditation, anger, I soon discovered that there was a great deal more going on during the longer periods of anger than could be covered by the word *anger*. I had believed, as I had been taught, that the experience of many hours of being upset about something in my meditation sittings was just made up of the arising and passing away of moments of anger that were wrongly apprehended as a self that was angry, and that if I could see anger as just the arising and passing away of these mind-moments, I would become free of it. From going through a few periods of meditating with angry feelings that lasted for several hours and noticing what it was I was indeed experiencing (instead of what I should be naming as the experience), I quickly saw that there were moments of fear, hurt, rage, loneliness, sadness, remorse, guilt, resentment, and so forth appearing throughout these long episodes. I began to see that there really was no hindrance of "pure" ill will—such a hindrance had to be composed of other feelings that interacted with each other and kept the whole thing going.

Still, I believed in many of the other narratives of Theravada Buddhism and found myself questioning one adopted belief after another for many months. I progressively loosened up my meditation practice to allow myself to think deeply about these beliefs and whether they were verifiable within my experience. No aspect of the Buddhist doctrine was immune from this type of examination. I questioned the validity of the Four Noble Truths, the three characteristics of existence (impermanence, suffering, and no-self), and whether liberation of mind is possible. I came to believe that as concepts, none of the teachings are true—they are just narratives to help people live more wholesome and happier lives. This is the direct opposite of what I started out believing.

One day I read this famous passage in the Lankavatara Sutra, a Mahayana text: "From the day of the Buddha's awakening to his final entering into nibbana, he did not proclaim a doctrine." This reverberated within my consciousness for days. It made sense to me. The Buddha did not teach a doctrine. He taught what he had experienced as a way for his mind to find peace and not get caught up in producing more pain for himself and others. His way was founded not on a system of right-sounding beliefs but on experiential knowledge. The truth of one's experience is the truth of the teaching. And the concepts about one's experiences are just the imperfect ways we have for thinking and talking about them. When I saw this, the Buddha's teaching began to make sense to me once again, for from having examined it to the point of abandoning it, I came to understand it anew from a completely different angle, from having unlearned the meditation practices and the concepts embedded in them that I had been taught.

It is from going through this process of transformative conceptualization, on multiple occasions with different impasses, that I have been able to develop this approach to unlearning meditation. It is not a procedure or strategy that you can employ—it is a skill (or process) you can learn and refine.

13

Effortless Calm

The process of getting into a calm state is fairly straightforward. It happens in meditation practice through watching the breath, using a mantra, or following a guided meditation. If you do any of these practices, your mind will eventually calm down and the disturbing, distracting thoughts will go away. What is there to unlearn here?

I didn't consider that there was anything to unlearn about calm states until I began questioning the whole notion of applying effort to become calm. When I was most agitated, anxious, or restless and I needed my mind to settle down, the effort to bring my attention to my breath would tend to have a frantic, pressured, and even desperate quality. It then came to me that the mind that was agitated was the same mind that was applying effort, so no wonder my attempts to hold awareness of the breath were forced and aggressive. That is how I act when agitated. I get impatient, and when I do something, I do it aggressively, not slowly or calmly as I would when more settled.

It's paradoxical to act slowly, calmly, and kindly when you're feeling restless, anxious, and impatient. For most people beginning meditation, a guided meditation that plants the ideas of "letting go of thoughts," "sinking into the body," "moving with the flow of the breath," relayed in a gentle, soothing voice seems to be the most direct way of cutting through the tension at the outset of a meditation sitting. Getting calm on your own by a bare, silent noticing of the breath may not be as easy as being led to the breath by a relaxed and reliable guide, though you may at times be your own guide, speaking to yourself in a way that helps you relax into the breath. Following the breath can in itself be quite relaxing, even hypnotic.

Many of the meditation practices people do for the purpose of calming the mind bear such a close resemblance to hypnosis that I wonder what the actual differences are. Certainly, a guided meditation meant to induce a trance state is not all that different from a verbal hypnotic induction, except for the fact that it lacks posthypnotic suggestions, but what about being aware of the breath at the nostrils or abdomen? Is that a hypnotic way of inducing a calm state?

The answer depends on the technique you use, how you use it, and what you experience.

Counting breaths, or noting them using labels like "breathing in" and "breathing out," is akin to hypnosis. You are adding words to the experience of breathing, often turning the breathing into something regular and rhythmic. You are also following the words just as much as you're following the breath, which fills and draws your attention more than just staying with the breath without using words or numbers. If you do this enough, you find your mind gets habituated to this procedure of calming. And generally, the calm state you experience is much the same each time. This way of inducing a calm state is fairly predictable and reliable, that is, unless you find yourself in a psychological space or physical environment where you just can't concentrate on breath and the words you use to note it. Then it not only may not work, but it may become a frustrating exercise, fraught with tension and ending in disappointment.

Rather than using words to stay focused on the breath, you may be taught to focus on the sensation of breathing as either the touch of air at the nostrils or the rise and fall of the abdomen or diaphragm. At first this may be accompanied by words, such as *in* and *out* or *ris-*

ing and *falling*, but you are attempting to be aware of the physical sensation of breathing, and so the words fade away and you just notice how the abdomen feels when it inflates and deflates, or how the breath brushes against your upper lip like a feather or enters your nose like a gentle breeze blowing through an open window. As you stay with the "natural breath" (as S. N. Goenka refers to it), you may find that it is uneven, and far from its being hypnotic, it can be both compelling and disturbing. Your attention is following something a bit more wild than the controlled and relaxing breathing that is tamed by words and concentration, which often requires even greater effort to stay with, especially since there are no words being planted in your experience, and you must sit with your thoughts intruding, distracting, judging. This is certainly not hypnosis.

Being with the natural breath in meditation may lead to calm states, but that is not its sole purpose—it can also lead to other kinds of meditative experiences. Breath meditation of this sort is thus taught as not just for the quieting of the mind but also for becoming aware of whatever you experience. When you begin a meditation sitting with this kind of awareness of the breath established, you may not know which way it will go: calm or otherwise. With the hypnotic forms of breath meditation, you pretty well know the direction in which your meditation sittings should go, for you are manipulating and influencing the meditation in that direction.

Now, there is a third way that your mind can get calm in meditation. You have already encountered it in the previous chapters and perhaps in your meditation sittings. It is effortless and just happens. There is no technique behind it. But that doesn't mean there's nothing for us to do. A good deal of unlearning is needed in order for us to truly trust and accept this other way of entering calm states in meditation.

Drifting Off and Waking Up

About fifteen years ago, I wrote an article with the title "Drifting Off and Waking Up" and published it in a small newsletter I was sending out at the time. In that article I tried to describe the benefits of letting ourselves drift off toward sleep in our meditation sittings. I will be doing the same, and a much better job of it, in the next few chapters. The basic idea is that when we truly allow ourselves to drift off in meditation, instead of falling asleep, we may find that we just graze the surface of sleep and emerge into a wakeful, tranquil state. If you allow yourself to be drowsy, rather than struggling against it, you may find yourself coming out the other end in a calm state of mind that has all the qualities of tranquil meditative states, because it is one. Here is an example from someone's journal.

> I became aware gradually that I was getting sleepy, although sleepy isn't the best word—maybe more relaxed. I thought "Thank goodness" because this usually means that soon I'll be less attached to the thoughts—they seem to happen without me thinking them. Which is what happened. I went into a dreamlike state. I was awake throughout as far as I know, although I can't remember too much, except that there was a dog talking to his vet about his treatment during one part. Another thing I remember, probably because it is so unusual, is very vivid images of moving quickly through a forest—probably because of a movie I'd watched the night before.

In fact, allowing drowsiness may result in states of mind people are told to avoid in meditation practice. I have met many meditators who have never allowed themselves to drift off in meditation and so have only briefly touched upon such experiences before abruptly bringing their attention back to some appropriate object of meditation, such as the breath. If the instructions in this book are your first exposure to meditation, you will probably find little resistance to drifting off and waking up in meditation. But if there is resistance to letting your mind drift where it will, then look at the resistance and be gentle with it.

I have already mentioned that this approach will threaten your need to control your mind, so it is quite natural to be afraid of any unbidden and unfamiliar state that arises. You might be inclined in some cases to meet these calm experiences with distrust, because they might be strange and disorienting. By accepting them and letting them progress as they will, you may begin to slowly develop trust in this paradoxical process of drifting off and waking up.

This way of entering calm states through staying with what you experience is not only a gentle, receptive way of settling the mind, but I believe it is also psychologically safer and more grounded than approaches that accelerate the process, such as practices that require long periods of sitting, focusing intently on objects, and moving energy through your body.

In addition to the difficulties inherent in trusting being open to our mind as it is in meditation, there is another, more worldly concern about how we appear to those around us as we meditate in a group setting. How you look to others as you sit on the cushion can affect your willingness to allow your mind to drift to the point of being okay with going toward sleep—because allowing that will likely lead to a slumping posture and drooping head. You won't look like the athletic, awake, and aware meditator found in magazine photos. As your chin slides down your chest and saliva forms at the corners of your mouth, you may feel a little embarrassed and uneasy at having taken my suggestions. And when you slip into a peaceful sleep only to be awakened by the sound of your own snoring, you may curse me under your breath and regret taking up this practice. I don't blame you. I understand this situation all too well.

We are part of a meditation culture that has certain values, of which this approach might seem to go against the grain by placing a value on staying with your experience over correct meditation posture. Though this brings up another point, that what I am calling an experience of drifting off and waking up is more commonly looked at as mind-wandering, fantasy, or daydreaming.

So not only am I advising you to practice what would be considered poor form in meditation sitting, but I am also telling you to be "unmindful" and "indulgent"—using some of the prevailing meditation culture's language. This may be a tougher hurdle for some of you to get over than the one allowing your posture to sag. It could seem that allowing your mind to drift in meditation is unproductive, self-indulgent, and lazy—that it will lead nowhere but to more daydreaming and fantasies. You would be falling asleep in meditation and have sittings where all you did was "space out." It wouldn't seem like much of a meditation practice, and certainly not one you would be proud of.

You can no doubt see why most meditation teachers don't teach what I am advocating here and why calming the mind is often taught from the point of view of instructions. With instructions to focus on an object of meditation, you can also have rules that are in accordance with the common perception of meditation: You sit with a straight back, fully awake, concentrating on the primary object of meditation. You don't let your back cave in, and you straighten up whenever a downward pull or slumping position is detected. You wake yourself up whenever sleepy. You keep your attention on the primary object and never stray from it. Now that sounds like meditation!

We can go in circles around these issues. I could try harder to convince you to trust the mind as it is in meditation. I could also direct criticism at instruction-based practices. But I could also defend instruction-based practices and give a knowledgeable critique of my own approach. These are basic debating skills of which many of us are capable. But no matter which side wins the debate, we might not be really convinced. At least, I wouldn't.

So let's move from ideas about meditation practice to the experiences of meditators. The initial instruction about bringing your attention to the touch of the hands, your rear against the cushion, or your body sitting can create conditions for your mind to slip into calm states. One thing that this simple instruction does is take your attention away from your head and torso, where we tend to locate thinking and feeling, and bring your awareness to a part of your body where much of your experience is just sensations unrelated to emotions. Also, focusing for any length of time on anything still, such as the body sitting, will naturally relax the mind and can make you drowsy.

The following example, taken from a woman who began Recollective Awareness Meditation several years ago, is one where the touch of hands is included in conjunction with other rhythmic, hypnotic objects.

> I felt the breath in my hands, actually my pulse, and heard the clock at the same rhythm. A few thoughts and some tension in my head with a sense of weightiness. I stayed with the hands and pulse a lot. Then there was a sudden shift to visions and poetry—snapshot scenes of canoeing in Canada and poem possibilities. Then a sudden shift to brilliant sparkles of colored lights, round bulbs on thin tubes, lasting for just a brief moment. Then undulating granular colors that came and went. It was restful, peaceful, and at times I would come back to the pulse in my hands and a witness viewpoint from within the body. Mind was untroubled, felt settled, calm, accepting, and a little spacey and tired, but gently so, not unpleasant—it was like a welcome respite—the bell startled me.

Once the meditator's mind got settled, she shifted to seeing images and colors and then to a poem she was working on, and her attention left the touch of the hands, her pulse, and the ticking of the clock. It is natural in these calm states to lose contact with what leads into the state and not to return to those objects of concentration. But if someone follows an instruction to keep returning to the breath or a mantra or a specific visualization, then the natural progression of the state is interrupted rather then furthered. The image of canoeing and the possibilities for a poem appear as new objects to focus on, and they are later replaced by brilliant sparkles of colored lights and the undulating granular colors. To go with those images and ideas, the meditator had to allow her attention to leave the pulse in her hands.

Because of the drowsiness associated with drifting into these calm inner spaces, many meditators fight these experiences, that is, until they find out that this is just what happens to most people who use these instructions. There was one student, several years ago, who never got the message that these instructions would lead to drifting off in meditation. That was because he was in prison and did not have access to a teacher's comments until he had sat this way for a few weeks. His journal records many instances of trying to ward off sleep, of not letting himself go with the drowsiness. The only time it was quiet enough for him to meditate was in the early morning, so he also saw that as contributing to his sleepiness.

The reason that sleepiness or drowsiness has been so attacked by some traditional approaches has its source in ancient Buddhist meditation manuals, in which ardent meditators are instructed to keep themselves awake using a variety of methods. Sleepiness was considered a hindrance to meditation. And yet, tranquillity was considered a state of mind worthy of cultivation. Experientially, when most people feel tranquil, they also feel a little sleepy. Unfortunately, the ideal that is presented to meditators is to be both tranquil and awake, which gets in the way of becoming tranquil first and more wakeful later.

14

Meditating with Drifting Off
and Waking Up

Meditating with this drifting-off and waking-up process is not always easy, nor is it straightforward. Many times we'll find ourselves in a tranquil state without remembering how we got there. It is as though the memory has been obliterated and we can't retrieve it. We don't know how it happened or what preceded what. All we know is that the thinking has changed or died down or vanished, and everything is calmer.

When we go into a calm state from a train of thought, it's usually hard to remember the transition. There is also often a loss of the content of the thinking and no memory of what was so important or compelling about it. Here is an example from a student's journal.

> The whole train of thought in the beginning seemed quite important. It suddenly and completely dropped off. I can remember nothing about what I had been thinking about and what mattered about it. I see how I am drawn into habitually making up conjectures about this—but actually am more amazed that it could drop like this.

The meditator is trying to understand why the thinking dropped, but since she has no memory of the transition, she has to conjecture why. This is one of the main problems we encounter when we don't have awareness of how things came about. We speculate about the causes and come up with a theory or explanation about how things happened, but we really don't know. We have no remembered experience to refer back to. So one of the reasons for remembering the transition is to get a clearer picture of how such elusive states actually arise within our sittings. From my perspective, it is important to get a glimpse of the conditions that give rise to these experiences in order to better understand these states, to use them, and to benefit from them.

We can often remember a transitional event when it is accompanied by an image or an energetic shift, as in this meditator's experience.

> I had a sensation in my abdomen, and then I saw a hand going under it, and then I get a gentle rush of energy up my body. That normally means I have transitioned into another state, where my mind is momentarily clear and tranquil.

In this kind of transition, you can be focused on the breath, on sounds, on body sensations, thoughts, emotions, images, or anything that comes into your awareness, even shopping lists or a song that keeps going around in your mind. You can't rule anything out as a possible way to enter into a tranquil state.

Staying with intense emotions often creates enough wakefulness at the outset for us to notice the transition to calmness. By tolerating your restlessness, agitation, anxiety, and craving, it is possible for something to be comprehended about what keeps them going, as found in this meditator's journal entry.

> After some time I feel restless as I begin to think of all the things I want to accomplish today, especially since I return to work tomorrow after a week away. I won't be able to get to everything, and I feel disappointed. I feel the urge to

get up from my seat and leave meditation so that I can start tackling my to-do list. I have the sudden thought that this could be an "attraction to sense experience" I hear some meditators speak about. I've usually thought this phrase or concept indicated something grosser, like the sensual pleasures of sex or eating, or soaking in a hot tub. Now I realize that the kind of busyness I'm thinking about is pleasurable to me—a sense of accomplishment, of mastery, a kind of order or beauty. With this awareness I begin to see a light purple or lilac color slowly appear in my mind's eye. It pulses in and out slowly, appearing at the center of its vaguely circular form, expanding outward toward some invisible rim, and then contracting back from rim to center again, in and out.

By making the connection between the kind of busyness the meditator is thinking about and sense pleasure, she has seen something about the hindrance of restlessness and its relation to other emotions. When such things are directly comprehended, the mind drops the hindrance and moves into a tranquil state. Seeing colors pulsating in meditation and following their movements and changes are an important feature of calm states for some people.

Describing Calm States

How we describe the calm states helps us become more aware of them. We really don't have adequate language for these experiences. By describing them in more detail, we can become aware of minor things about them that we normally would not consider all that valuable.

People tend to describe visual images more readily than purely mental processes, primarily because they are more memorable. There are many people who do not see visual images or colors in their sittings and become focused on sensations, sounds, or ideas instead of images. These details may be a bit harder to remember afterward, being subtler and not necessarily what you might be accustomed to recollecting. I will often ask students if they were aware of a certain texture or tone or way of perceiving things in these states. The sitting described below is an example of someone noticing the texture of her mind (as well as visual images, types of thinking, and level of awareness).

> Sinking deeper into meditation. Sinking has a familiar textural feel: thick, soft, enveloping. Loose thoughts continue, but I'm not very interested in them; they are nonsensical and flowing as I continue to sink. This culminates in an image of a cow's face chewing hay and a lightening in the depth of the field so that I am in a more aware spot. I wonder where this image came from and I remember a conversation with a dear friend in which I stated that I was happy on farms. This cycle of sinking with loose, unconnected thoughts happens twice more (each ended in an image, but I can't remember the images) and a lightening of the depth to a more aware spot.

These are the kinds of description that sensitize us more to the direct experience of our mind in such states. The meditator's description of her thoughts is part of the description of the state she is in and not separate from it. So when she writes that her thoughts are loose, nonsensical, and flowing, she is recognizing how thinking functions in that particular state, even though she does not recall the content of the thoughts. If she were able to recollect the content of the thoughts, even just a word or a phrase or the theme, that would add some more detail to her experience.

Trying to intentionally recall things in these calm states can add too much pressure and be counterproductive. At a recent retreat, after listening to a student's description of seeing a particular image in his sittings, I suggested that he focus on the details of similar images when they arise.

> Unfortunately, last night Jason took me aside and told me to look for things. It upset my balance. There was a bit more effort and tightness. Some pain has come back—the tasking

of it. And probably some doubt. I've got to stop jumping on or waiting for visual images. So silly to be tense. It spoils all the fun and clarity of it. Still see some stuff and there were times of relaxation.

We really need to have a gentle awareness of what is going on when we are in a calm space. Attempts to do things in an active and directed manner often get in the way and may snap us out of it. That is another reason why remembering what goes on in these states afterward is so helpful. By just letting ourselves be subjected to what is going on in the calm state without trying to be too awake or too directing and controlling, we get to experience it more thoroughly, more deeply. And recollecting it builds up our awareness of it. When that kind of state arises again, it is likely that we will be a bit more aware than we were before, and that awareness may lead to further discernment within the state and finer distinctions between other, similar states.

Part of what we may then become aware of is how a particular calm state has changed over time. Many times we may not really notice the change until we put it into words, as happened in the following example.

> I used to call this experience "quivering," but it now feels like a very fluid state. I have a sense of these layers that I experience being like an airplane moving through different air currents.

Describing the Order of Events

Our sense of time is not very accurate when in an extended calm space. I have often heard people remark about how short sittings seem. Most meditators find that meditating for more than an hour is not difficult when this happens, and so they can easily increase the length of their sittings. Just as these states alter our sense of how much time has passed, they can affect how we see things happening in time. They can throw off our sense of a linear ordering of events.

There is a vague image of moving through pillars—very misty and floaty. There is also the sense of moving toward an opening. There is a knowing of an instant of fear, and again the whole thing vanishes. In this one, I questioned the sense of order. I almost felt as if the whole thing had happened before the visualizations and they were simply the later representations of the process.

The meditator is alluding to having experienced a different ordering of events than what her mind recalls as the linear steps in the process. She recalls (1) an image of moving through pillars, (2) moving toward an opening, (3) an instant of fear, and (4) a vanishing of the fear and everything else that was happening. But what she feels is that the fear and its vanishing happened before seeing the image of moving through pillars and toward an opening.

One of the reasons we can get confused about the order of events in such states as the one described above is that calm states can cause us to experience things in a multilinear way. This experience of multilinearity is not the same as experiencing things happening simultaneously. The difference is that there are two or more linear progressions that your mind is engaged in that don't seem to relate to each other. They are progressing on their own steam and may not meet up. In the example above, the meditator's mind may have been on one track of experiencing fear and on another track of moving through pillars. This kind of split between following one track of feeling and another of imagery is not uncommon. What often creates confusion is when one of the tracks stops while the other continues on. We may then, in our memory, try to condense them into one linear progression of experience, especially if we have a strong view that all of our mental experience goes in a single straight line.

The Unexpected

Calm states have a tendency to confound our expectations for them. Unexpected things happen in them, and happen afterward from our having been in them. There are some common patterns that I can illustrate for you, but here we are also entering an area where individuals generally have experiences that are particular to them.

It is this unexpected and idiosyncratic aspect of certain calm states that can lead to wariness of them. We tend to doubt experiences that don't match anything we have ever heard about, or act differently from the ideas we have about how they should be. For instance, you may believe that after being in a deep, calm space for a while in a meditation sitting, you should be relaxed and serene afterward. When you aren't, you may be alarmed by that. Some people do experience a pattern of emerging from a calm state to find themselves anxious or restless.

I have listened to many accounts of people having a calm meditation sitting in the morning, only to find themselves touchy, anxious, or angry when they get to their job or class or do their errands later. There are other factors involved, of course, but when these same individuals have switched to meditating in the afternoon or evening, some of the extra emotional vulnerability and reactivity they were experiencing during the day vanishes. It is often a difficult choice to decide not to sit in the morning when that is the best time for you, and especially if you tend to have calm or pleasant sittings then. Some people resist the suggestion to sit later in the day or at night because there is usually more mental activity and emotions from the day.

You may wonder why I suggest breaking this pattern. On a retreat lasting a few days and nights, the vulnerability or agitation that can surprisingly come over you after these calm states can be gone through in an environment where you can sit with the experience and get to know it. Out in the world, especially at work or in a class, you are put in a position of having to suppress and manage the difficult feelings and anxiety, and your work, studies, and relationships may suffer on account of it.

You may start to get the picture that arriving at calmness in meditation is not all that reliably pleasant. For a while it relieves pain; then, at another time, it seems to intensify our experience of pain. Here is an example of a baffling experience around physical pain.

> Several discreet points in meditation where I drop into a deeper place. I cannot describe it, but it is very clear in the meditation. I am fighting off an infection and do not feel very well physically. It is interesting to me that one time when I drop into a deeper place the pain is more acute, another time I drop into a deeper place I cannot perceive the pain. I see how I feel compelled to make up something definitive about what happens when dropping into deeper places and what happens with the senses. It is not definitive like that in my experience.

When I read reports like this one it does make me question our ideas about, and attitudes toward, calm states of mind. This meditator would like to make a definite statement about what happens all of the time when she drops into a deeper place, such as, "pain always goes away," but she can't honestly do that when her experience won't corroborate it.

Exploring Calm States

Exploring calm states requires us to think about them and to put language to our experiences the best we can. We often don't think about what is going on when we are in a calm meditative state—we tend to go along with the pleasure, sinking more into it, rather than trying to activate our mind to reflect on the process. Sometimes we can't think while in one of these states, as some of them are free from thinking. But our awareness of those kinds of experience can still benefit from some reflection on them when we emerge from them and can once again think. Then there are times when thinking about the experience interrupts it, and there are other times when it doesn't. Here is a student's exploration of a type of calm state he has become familiar with. He is exploring it in the sitting itself, but since it is being recollected in a journal after the sitting, there are also elements of discernment of the state after the fact.

> Most of the sit was very quiet with brief punctuations of thinking semiverbal thoughts (mostly random fragments very vaguely related to content, like the sit or people I know). These thoughts didn't disturb the silence, but there was a general sense of observing them and wanting to look for connections to emotion or body, which did disturb the silence. Noticed several kinds of silence: (1) spacious nonvisual area in front of awareness, sometimes deep, sometimes very flat or shallow; (2) solid stillness that seemed frozen so much that this was a bit startling and threatening; (3) quiet random visual activity that was well delineated and detailed but more geometric than representational. Occasionally checked in with tingling, which was subtle, bright, and continuous—sometimes it seemed like the tingling around the face/head was correlated with quiet. Tried to characterize emotional state, but this seemed rather flat (peaceful, and maybe happy, but not dramatically so); curiosity seemed to be the dominant emotion, but questioned whether that is an emotion.

He notices that the thoughts (random fragments) don't disturb the silence, but the task of making connections within his experience does. He identifies three kinds of silence. The first, being spacious and deep, fits almost everyone's idea of a what a silent state of mind would be. The other two are more unusual. The second is a kind of threatening frozen state of mind, while the third is accompanied by random visual images. These experiences arise while he is calm, and yet they have a more active quality. His exploration continues beyond a delineation of the silence to looking at his emotional state within the various calm states. He sees his emotional state as flat but on reflection wonders if it may just be peaceful or a low-level happiness. His question about curiosity being an emotion is a good one for meditators. It is a quality of interest in one's experience, which carries with it a certain energy, so why wouldn't it be an emotion?

His exploration touches on many aspects of his experience, such as what he saw, how he felt, or what the experience meant to him. It is interesting to note that he looks at the nature of thinking, seeing two types of thoughts in this experience, one that is arising randomly and the other that is trying to make connections. This sort of experience is seldom explored, especially if there is a belief that the calm states you experience in meditation should be free of thinking.

And How Is All of This Useful?

I often get asked about the value and use of allowing these calm states to continue, and I reply with what I have observed as the virtues at the time and the benefits seen afterward. At the time, there can be freedom from your ordinary thoughts and cares. Whatever anger, fear, or craving may have been on your mind, it is generally absent in these states or is but a whisper. There is a way your mind slows down and your body relaxes that can be pleasurable and restorative. And when lights, colors, images, sounds, or sensations come into awareness, your mind may be able to focus on them with sharpness and clarity.

Afterward you might feel refreshed, without pressures and worries. You may feel a bit lighter. Sometimes you may feel a bit spacey and disoriented. Still, you might notice that your mood has softened and that you are less reactive.

You don't need to take my word for it. You can test it out for yourself.

15

Drifting to Absorption

I am going to introduce a new term, the Pali/Sanskrit word *samadhi,* to discuss the states of mind that develop out of this process of drifting off and waking up. In John Grimes's *Concise Dictionary of Indian Philosophy,* he gives multiple definitions of *samadhi* from both the Hindu and Buddhist traditions. He starts with a general definition: concentration; absorption; a calm, desireless fixity; a unifying concentration. The Hindu tends to elevate *samadhi,* considering such states to be "superconscious," "transcendent," "inexpressible," and at times, "free of thought and mental activity." The Buddhists will tend to agree with this assessment for the more refined and developed *samadhi* states, called *jhana,* but will also use the term *samadhi* when talking about calm states of mind within the reach of most individuals. Thus there are preliminary *samadhi* states, which would not be called *samadhi* by Yogic practitioners but are nonetheless necessary for people's minds to move into the more developed and purified *jhanas.*

These preliminary *samadhi* states, unnamed in the Pali Discourses of the Buddha (though they are later designated by the name of "access" *samadhi* in Buddhist commentarial literature), are aptly described in progressions such as the following:

"Having seen oneself overcome the five impediments [to calmness of mind], joy arises within one. From feeling joy, there is a quiet elation. With one's mind elated, one's body becomes peaceful. Being with the peacefulness of one's body causes an experience of profound happiness. One's consciousness experiencing such happiness enters *samadhi*" (Samannaphala Sutta, Digha Nikaya).

Such descriptions leave out the "drifting off" side of the drifting-off–waking-up experience and place it under the impediment often archaically translated as "sloth and torpor." By highlighting the wakefulness found in experiences of joy, elation, peace, and happiness, many people have assumed that the preliminary *samadhi* states have to be entirely wakeful and that any sleepiness gets in the way. But that is actually not the case, according to a prior passage in this same discourse: "When abandoning laziness in one's body and mind, one sits with laziness in the distance; and while perceiving inner lights, with awareness and discernment [of one's experiences], one cleanses one's mind of laziness."

Here we have the drifting-off and waking-up experience rather succinctly described. It is a preliminary *samadhi* state, what I will be calling a pre–*jhanic* state. The Buddha says that one has a perception of inner lights, which are used as a means to overcome laziness and thus produce more wakefulness. Focusing on such lights and images is the direction the Buddha himself endorsed, rather than trying to stop the hypnagogic state from forming.

Hypnagogic States

Hypnagogic (or hypnogogic) states are generally experienced during the transition from waking to sleep. But they may not necessarily occur every time we fall asleep. They also may occur but leave no memory, as they tend to be difficult to recall afterward. There are times when we are more aware, more conscious, in these hypnagogic states, and when that occurs we may experience certain phenomena.

The visual imagery often consists of random speckles, geometrical patterns, and representational images, which may be monochromatic or colored, still or in motion, flat or three-dimensional, but are usually fleeting and given to rapid changes. There can also be other sense-door experiences in the mind. Verbal thoughts are generally incomplete sentences that don't make much sense, though there can be wordplay or poetry that appears to convey meaning. Sometimes the thoughts are in one's own voice, while other times the thoughts are in other people's voices. And of course, one can hear music, bells, and other common sounds. There can also be odors, fragrances, tastes, and bodily sensations, such as tingling and numbness. The external sense objects that would normally be a part of such sense experiences are absent, though at times the experience seems so real that people feel a need to know if there is, for instance, light shining in their eyes, bells being rung outside, or real flowers or incense in the room.

There are a few other features that are quite common meditative experiences. One is the often disconcerting experience of perceiving your body to be larger than it is or losing the sensation of a certain part of your body. Another is the rather pleasant feeling of floating or moving effortlessly through space. And yet another is the experience meditators often have of falling forward and returning to awareness with a full-body jerk.

As you can see, there is a good deal of similarity between the phenomena experienced in hypnagogic states and some of the states described in the journal entries of those who are drifting off and waking up in meditation. Hypnagogic states have been used in modern times to develop out-of-body experiences and lucid dreaming, and yet here we are using them to develop tranquillity and insight in meditation. As pre-*jhanic* states, hypnagogic states are developed differently than they would be to achieve specific ends like out-of-body travel, lucid dreaming, or psychic abilities. It is interesting to note in this context, however, that the Buddhist teachings on psychic abilities, out-of-body travel, and other paranormal feats state that they can come about through practicing the *jhanas*.

This is certainly a different way to develop *jhanas* than found in more traditional teachings, which advocate concentrating on a single object, such as an image or mantra, and warn against letting the mind drift. It sounds contradictory that by allowing fragmentation and wandering, the mind eventually becomes focused and concentrated. But that is how it is. Having developed these states in meditation over the years, I and many of my students are able to rather quickly pass through, or even bypass, the hypnagogic imagery, disconnected thoughts, and perceptual distortions and move into a more wakeful steady state. There can even be alert, wakeful transitions into the more steady and aware *samadhi* state, as it no longer requires the experience of drifting off in order to occur, though there is still a shift of attention, accompanied by an experience of letting go of your previous state of mind and being drawn into the newly arisen calm state.

Visuals in *Pre*-jhanic Samadhi *States*

The function of visual images in these pre-*jhanic samadhi* states, whether they are lights, colors, or pictures, is to draw your attention toward them. Sometimes an image appears in our mind and we move toward it, like a zoom lens bringing an image closer. At other times, an image fills our mind and we are in it, like seeing a painting or mural up close and being absorbed in it. Then there are those times when images and colors move and change, and our attention follows them.

Here is an example from a woman who is quite familiar with these experiences, having experienced them for many years in her practice.

I become aware of two flashlight-type beams way in the distance. The beams are moving around, and I have a sense that they are looking for me. I feel a friendliness and sweetness about them and keep looking at them. The searchlights continue toward my position and become bigger with the continued sweeping effect of the lights. When they get so close to me that they almost fill the field, they easily morph into my familiar swirls of colors, and I know I'm back home in familiar territory.

It may be difficult to avoid trying to find some kind of meaning in visual images and lights. If you are someone who interprets symbols and sees meaning in colors and shapes, then you will tend to do that with the visual imagery. You may just have to let that go on in your sittings and not try to stop it. Who knows, you may get some kind of insight from your interpretation of an image. But in the process, you might also find that you have stopped the preliminary *samadhi* state from going further.

It is quite common to have certain progressions of visual experience. One such progression is seeing a light or color and then seeing a picture that features the same color or radiance. The following journal entries are from a woman who has extraordinary recall of visual images in her sittings.

A bald-headed man dressed in white, in a white room with very bright sunlight pouring in. No contrast, a bit like a whiteout. He was blowing on a suspended white paper cup that was in front of his face.

In this instance, the image of a bald man and the white paper cup arises with a white room with light pouring in. As the meditator describes it, there is nothing but whiteness in her visual field. In my own experience, I would often see a white expanse of light and then an image form within it as I stayed with it. Sometimes the image would be of clear, radiant water, while at other times the images would be of a more random nature, akin to this bald man dressed in white blowing on a white paper cup.

There does appear, in meditation circles at least, to be a bias against these random, unusual images and a preference for images that can be found in certain texts or teachings on meditation. I believe dividing images in this way creates judgment about your experience, as if the truth of the experience lies in the correctness of the image and not in its other significant qualities. If you feel genuine peace and joy along with mental clarity from having been absorbed in a bizarre image, then that is a valid experience of peace, joy, and clarity. To then devalue it because it wasn't a "correct" image from your tradition is giving far too much weight to the meaning of the image over the beneficial aspects of your experience of the samadhi state.

In these pre-*jhanic* states, the images that draw us in are the ones that interest us at that moment. Such images can't be decided on beforehand. We only know that we are interested in them when they appear to us. Some people have a tendency to see the same types of recurring images, while others may experience a tremendous variety. The person with the journal entry of the bald man is one of those who tend to experience unusual images, many of which appear to be based on memories. Here is an example of the development in a meditation sitting of an image that came from the same person's memory.

My two younger sisters are turning the rope for double Dutch. I was trying to teach a friend how to jump into the two ropes with the timing of one rope down on the ground and the other rope in the sky. It was too confusing for my friend to do it this way. I showed her how to stand in the center of the two ropes and jump each time a rope touched the ground—it was about following a certain rhythm. I suggested she move to the left and to the right—and feel that meeting place between two worlds. She still could not feel the rhythm. My grandfather came and said, "Just listen to the sound of the rope and do not watch it." She started jumping, and we all started to cheer.

At first glance, this type of experience can appear to be a re-lived memory. The meditator's mind is using a memory that has arisen of its own in order to find something to focus on. The two ropes are moving in a rhythm, alternating up and down, the girl is moving left and right, but at first that movement is not coordinated with the rhythm of the ropes. Then an idea arose in the guise of a memory of the meditator's grandfather, to focus on the sound of the ropes and not the image of them. The sound is another rhythm, as is jumping rope, and so there was a way it all came together for her. This seems to have produced a type of rhythmic imagery that could come up again and carry her into a more absorbed state in a later sitting.

> I saw a close-up view of double Dutch ropes being turned and felt my hands had become enormous. My hands were in the foreground, opening as they moved forward and becoming crescent moons as I pulled them back. Back and forth to the rhythm of the two ropes moving through space. I just stayed here feeling the rhythm of the ropes and my hands guiding me into this space, knowing how to enter. I then felt surrounded by the two ovals of the ropes and the rhythm of moving slightly to the left and right, staying here forever, until the rope turners were tired.

Here the meditator's mind could keep the motion of the two jump ropes and the rhythm of jumping going for an extended period. The imagery of the ropes and the way of moving with them had been developed in earlier sittings, and now it just comes to her quite effortlessly. Her mind has learned how to follow the imagery and become absorbed in it. This is a much more realistic and natural use of visual imagery than is commonly found in the more orthodox meditation manuals, where the direction is often to fix one's attention on a stationary image. Our experience, especially our thinking, is not stationary. It is moving all the time. Thus it is quite natural to follow moving imagery, changing colors and forms, and shifting intensities and opacities of light.

There are so many varieties of visual experience in these pre-*jhanic* states that I can't cover them all in this chapter. But there is one more I'll mention that is fairly common. It is when one image quickly follows upon another in a way that doesn't seem to make any sense whatsoever. We can usually handle the odd random image with a surprised "Where did that come from?" But a succession of unrelated and unusual images can leave us wondering about our mental health. It is normal, however, in some of these pre-*jhanic* states, so don't worry. In fact, they can be quite integrating and beneficial when they're allowed. Here is an example from another one of the previous meditator's sittings.

I feel myself contained within this daylight oval space with a growing heaviness within my body. Sinking into something. Then a series of fleeting images, quick flashes—the residue of two orange canoes in a two-dimensional space, vibrating with a certain fuzziness, one on top of the other, the top canoe a bit to the left of the bottom one. The background shifting maroon, an aloe vera gel bottle underneath a counter, a bicycle stuck in an adobe wall, not as if it had crashed but that it had been embedded there for years. The words "sorting in rather than sorting it out."

16

Questions Surrounding *Samadhi*

Those of you new to learning about *samadhi* are probably unaware that there are several questions surrounding the topic of *jhanas* in Theravada Buddhist circles. It is not the purpose of this book to give my answers to certain questions and then try to explain and defend my point of view on what is a *jhana* and what isn't. What I have written regarding pre-*jhanic* states is as far as I am willing to go.

As much as *jhanas* can be defined, listed, and described in texts or talked about by meditation teachers, they must be experienced in order to be known. A concept or description won't convey what the experience is like to someone who has never experienced it, and for that reason I haven't commented on any of the journal entries as to what experiences in them might be *jhanas*.

Regarding particulars of the experience of a *jhana,* there are questions in these four areas:

1. Whether someone is breathing in a *jhana* or not
2. Whether there is awareness of the body and sense impressions or not

3. Whether a *jhana* is short-lived, as in a momentary flash, or lasts longer than a few seconds
4. Whether a *jhana* is an accessible experience for most meditators or is highly advanced and largely inaccessible

My response to these points is a philosophical one: A *jhana* does not arise from nowhere, nor does it create itself. It does not exist in a separate world, reality, or universal consciousness. It is not eternal. It is not a being, an entity, or a substance. It is a state of consciousness, like any other, and thus comes about through causes and conditions.

One of the main conditions is pre-*jhanic samadhi* states. A *jhana* is grown like a plant from a seed that has the right soil, enough water and sun, and grows in an appropriate climate according to the seasons. Other conditions include your morals and behavior, awareness and discernment, ability to focus and concentrate, and the effectiveness of your meditation practice to wear down the impediments to calm states of mind.

The Split between Samatha (Jhana *Practice*) *and Vipassana*

Most Vipassana teachers discourage the development of *jhanas,* warning students against them. "You will become attached to them" is how it is often put. Without the necessary wisdom to see how *jhanas* are mentally constructed, it is believed that Vipassana students will be led away from the path of insight and go down the road of seeking only bliss and happiness in meditation. Students are therefore only deemed ready to practice *jhana* when they have sufficient insight so as not to be deluded by these peaceful and purifying states of mind. The Vipassana goal is final liberation; *jhanas* are considered a temporary liberation that masquerades as the end of suffering but is nothing more than a pleasant resting place, a refreshing oasis in the scorching desert.

In response to that, those who teach the *jhanas* often go back to the Buddha's discourses, in which final liberation through the practice of *jhanas* is spoken of far more commonly than is liberation through strict *Vipassana*. The *jhanas* are extolled. They are a vehicle for seeing into erroneous views and purifying the mind. The initial four *jhanas* are even included in the Noble Eightfold Path and are thus seen as essential for a person's development on the path to final liberation.

Each side is right from its own perspective. Though I disagree with the tendency of certain Vipassana teachers to devalue *jhanas,* their concern about people being drawn into the pleasurable worlds of the *jhanas,* and taking those experiences as liberated states, is nonetheless valid. Though I agree with valuing *samadhi* and its cultivation in meditation practice, I do question the methods, theories, and observations of most of those who teach the *jhanas.*

What I do believe, for what it is worth, is that we don't have enough control over our path of meditation to say that we are exclusively practicing *Samatha* (calming, emptying, focusing) or *Vipassana* (noticing, discerning, exploring). We move from one to the other and back again. To use my language, sometimes we are with impasses, practicing awareness and discernment as found in *Vipassana,* while at other times we are in calm spaces, practicing ways to develop our inner peace and increasing our capacity to focus.

PART THREE

Multiple
Meditative Processes

17

A Theory of the Meditative Process

When I first came up with my theory of the meditative process, I saw it as primarily addressing the question of transformation in meditation. A few months later, after I had written and lectured on this theory, I saw that it addressed a much more basic question: What is meditation?

This is a question everyone asks. It is also one of those questions you can forget to ask after some years of meditating, when it has become quite obvious to you what meditation is: It is the meditation practice you use. If you sit and watch the breath, then meditation is sitting and watching the breath. It is that simple. But what about all those "other" meditation practices where people don't watch the breath? Are they also "real" meditation?

Instead of working on a narrow definition of meditation, I worked on one that would include all meditation practices (in truth, as many as would fit in the definition). What do all meditation practices have in common? The intention to meditate. The definition "meditation is what happens when you act upon the intention to meditate" is one that could be applied to almost every meditation practice that people learn. But then, there are always those questions

that irk most traditional meditation teachers, ones like, "When I listen to music, I go into a meditative state. Isn't that meditation?"

Here's a case where the definition of meditation as "what happens when you act upon the intention to meditate" might not
work. The person is intending to listen to music, not meditate, and
since he or she happens to go into a meditative state while doing
so, the person thus rightly wonders if that is meditation.

There has to be some way for the definition of meditation to
include both the intentional application of a technique or method
and the experiences of a meditative sort that come about uninten-
tionally. This distinction relates back to where I began this book,
with the tension between *the meditation instructions you use* and *your
mind as it is.* That our mind can find "meditative" states and understandings without doing an intentional practice is certainly within
the realm of people's experience. We could then say, "the experience
of meditation defines what meditation is." I would personalize that
definition, since meditative experience is individual, inward, subjective, and relative. So what we then have is the definition that has appeared on my Web site for the past decade or so, "One's experience
of meditation defines what meditation is (for oneself)."

That definition takes intentional meditation practices out of
the privileged position of being the standard-bearer. The practice of observing the breath, for example, is no longer what you
measure your practice by. The practice is now assessed by your
own experience of observing the breath, either in response to
the use of a technique or quite spontaneously. For instance, if
your experience of staying with the breath has been one great
struggle much of the time, then that is what that meditation
practice has been for you. You might argue that when you do
that practice well, you're meditating, while at other times you
are trying to meditate. But that once again puts the technique
into the position of defining what meditation is. When you look
at it from the vantage point of your experience of watching the
breath, there is really no absolutely right or wrong way of doing
it. There is just your experience of doing it the way you are do-

ing it. This shift in vantage point enables you to examine any of the practices you do, instead of evaluating yourself on how well you do that practice.

If meditation is defined by your experience of it, what then is the meditative process? Here is where my theory comes in. There is no single meditative process. By process I mean two things: (1) a particular way our minds function and (2) a particular way in which we relate to our experience. Let's just take it as granted in our meditation sittings that our minds do not always function in the same way, nor do we always relate to our experiences in the same fashion. We might assume that a meditative process should be calm, unemotional, focused, and mindful (or any combination of similar "meditative" qualities) and that when an unusual experience occurs we relate to it without reacting or judging or thinking about it for too long. That may be our experience for a part of a meditation sitting, but not for an entire sitting and certainly not for all of our sittings.

If we look honestly at our experiences in meditation, we'll see several types of meditative process, not just one. That is where my theory begins. I came up with six meditative processes, although I acknowledge that there could be more (theories about the operations of the human mind, especially when they rely on subjective experience, as this one does, cannot be set in stone).

Before I introduce the six meditative processes of my theory, there is a particular way of talking about them that you need to understand. When talking about a meditative process, I am essentially referring to *your mind as it is.* So when using *generative process,* I am referring to the mind being in a generative state, capable of creating and prone to building. When talking about a type of meditation practice, I am essentially referring to *the meditation instructions you use.* So when I state that something is a "generative practice," I am saying that when doing such a practice, you're instructed to create, generate, and build. This distinction between *process* and *practice* is maintained throughout my discussion of the meditative process.

The six meditative processes are as follows:

The Three Basic Meditative Processes

- The Receptive Process
- The Generative Process
- The Conflicted Process

The Three Developed Meditative Processes

- The Explorative Process
- The Non–Taking-Up Process
- The Connected Process

We begin our meditation practices with the first three types of meditative process dominating our sittings. As we continue to meditate, the three more-developed processes begin to make more of an appearance. They not only indicate that development has occurred in meditation but also become what is primarily developed.

After I created this model, I soon realized that it was a useful framework for talking about how meditation practices work. Along with that, I saw from how people began to use this theory that it is *not* very useful as a new labeling system. I want to emphasize that it is best to use this model as a way of gaining a perspective on meditation practice and experience, not to turn these processes into new names (or designations) for experiences you have in meditation.

The Receptive Process

This process is the cornerstone of unlearning meditation. It occurs when you're open and receptive to your thoughts, feelings, sensations, and perceptions in meditation. But it is not wholly perfect, since when you're receptive, you also experience resistance in the form of not wanting to be led, or swallowed up, by certain feelings, trains of thought, or unusual states of mind. We may even find ourselves more receptive to certain experiences sometimes and less so at other times, even though we remain in a receptive process. The process is found in how we permit our experience to go on as it is, regardless of any ideas we get about changing it by doing something else, such as a meditation instruction. We may even be ambivalent about letting it go on, and yet we do, finding that the receptive process has its own way of working.

So let's use this theory to address some of the questions you may have regarding unlearning meditation in relation to other meditation practices you have learned. What is really different about unlearning meditation compared with more traditional approaches to meditation?

First of all, unlearning meditation tends to be contrary to what one would rationally expect a meditation practice to be. It often results in doing the opposite of what is commonly taught as meditation. Could it be that unlearning meditation is based on different meditative processes from more traditional practices? That it is even perhaps the opposite of those practices?

If that were the case, then unlearning meditation would be as simple as making a rule to do the opposite of whatever you were trained to do. But it's not that simple. You have to be doing a meditation practice in order to observe what is going on for you in it. What is going on in unlearning meditation is a shift in the process you're using to do your "learned" meditation practice. Initially it is the same practice, more or less, it's just that you're relating to it differently.

This is where the receptive process becomes a helpful concept. When we relate to our experiences receptively, we let them wash over us, even carry us along. We may have some resistance to being pulled in one direction or pushed in another and want to hold our ground. It is natural to resist some of the experiences that come upon us when we are open and receptive. That's why something like pure acceptance, or being completely allowing, is more an idealized state of mind than an actual experience of what it is like when we are receptive. Even receptivity can be painful and unpleasant, and it is certainly chaotic at times. Just letting your mind roll on and on without stopping it is difficult to tolerate—but that is what receptivity is. It is not some ideal flow of experience that is always pleasurable, peaceful, or optimal.

To meet our familiar meditation practices with receptivity is to let them go on as they will while not getting caught up with fueling that process. That would be a different process, the generative process, which I will get to shortly. When doing any meditation instruction within the receptive process, you lose the sense of doing the instruction and take on the sense of experiencing the instruction.

For example, let's say you've constantly brought your attention back to the breath as your main meditation practice. As a consequence of this, you haven't let any thoughts or feelings remain for long. And you've probably deemed this particular way of meditating to be the way to meditate. Then you encounter this book, read many passages in disbelief, but find something in it persuasive enough to incline you to try some of it out, such as the instruction to sit with awareness of the touch of the hands while allowing thoughts and feelings into the meditation sitting. In a single stroke, this instruction allows you to break the habit of always returning to the breath; it allows you to let your thoughts and feelings remain and persist; and it causes you to question your assumption that breath awareness is the only way to meditate. So even if you do return to the breath on occasion, that practice occurs within a larger context of being receptive to other dimensions of experience. Within this receptive mode you are actually experiencing things about that practice rather than doing the practice. You perhaps see how you were using the breath to manage or avoid difficult feelings, or you might pick up on how awareness of breathing and thinking cannot really coexist when you force your attention solely on the breath.

The Generative Process

Meditation techniques that utilize the generative process are ones where the student is instructed to generate particular experiences or states of mind. Such practices as *metta* meditation, in which you try to produce a state of loving-kindness, are generative in this way. In these kinds of practice, the act of generating is given high importance—just stumbling upon a state of loving-kindness is not granted the same status as arriving at it through doing the appropriate formal meditation practice. The emphasis is thus on how to develop the ability to generate such states in times when you need them.

Meditation practices where the idea is to "generate an original state" are also generative, but in a different way. These practices often have a concept attached to them that the original state is the "truth," the "essence," or the "way things are." A good example of this is practicing awareness of the breath with the belief that by bringing your attention constantly back to the breath, the "pure" (original) state of mind that is fully awakened will be realized. But this is still generative. You're trying to create a state of mind that you have been told is an ultimate (or optimal) state. This way of thinking about the truth of your experience leads to a whole slew of practices that on the surface appear to open one up to "reality" but, in practice, are geared to producing experiences that you take as being ultimately real.

Then there are the several kinds of guided forms of meditation, which are undoubtedly generative, just because of the fact that someone else is giving verbal directions. Even if such meditations guide you to a certain place and then stop, leaving you to just sit with what comes up, it is still a generative practice.

And last of all, there are meditation practices that involve sending thoughts or feelings to others and receiving the same. Most who do such practices feel that they are sending "true" feelings and receiving the same back. This is the case with most generated emotions. When we have generated them successfully, we may then believe that is how we now feel about someone. Granted, there may be occasions when that is so, but for the most part, generated feelings give us a taste of what it would be like rather than the real thing. For example, generating loving-kindness for someone we despise doesn't mean that we'll no longer despise that person at times when he or she behaves in ways that we find despicable in real life or that all memories of how awful that person was to us have been obliterated by the loving feelings we temporarily knew in the guided meditation.

Generally, the generative process is a process of doing. It relies on effort, on concentration, and on persistence. The effort can be harsh and aggressive, though people can learn to be gentler with it. The type of concentration is often directed onto one thing at a time, one project or goal at a time. The persistence required to maintain such concentration and effort is often understated in such practices, but without it, people would give up on the ones that don't work for them much sooner than they do. Such determination is not necessarily a beneficial quality for everyone, and it can easily inhibit you from trying other possible directions.

Unlearning meditation, as a beginning meditation practice, doesn't use the generative process until other processes have become more established. When someone with an already existing meditation practice transitions through unlearning meditation, the person does it by doing the generative practices she or he has learned within a different meditative process. Beginning and transitioning meditators will engage both the receptive and the conflicted processes and will start to see generative practices from that angle.

The Conflicted Process

The conflicted process occurs when experiences are related to in a manner of trying to get rid of them. Thus, whenever there is internal struggle, tightfisted control, and great resistance, the conflicted process is functioning.

In most instances, a conflicted process arises when you try to do a generative practice and *your mind as it is* just won't let you do it. If you stick to the generative practice while in the conflicted process, the situation often gets worse, becoming more tense, pressured, painful. By holding on tightly to the generative instructions while not in a generative process, you just create more internal conflict. The way to transition around this conflict is to drop the generative practice and take up a receptive one as a way to enter the receptive process.

But engaging in a receptive process is not all that easy either. It can have its own forms of resistance, as you may have experienced by now. You may have found yourself fighting against going with your thoughts and feelings for long periods of the sitting, wanting to get rid of them or have them die down to some kind of manageable murmur. That too is conflicted. On the one hand you are accepting of whatever your mind does, and on the other, you want it to cooperate with a notion of how the meditation sitting should be and where it should go.

It is difficult to stay with the conflicted process without wanting to get rid of it—which is precisely what keeps it going. In the conflicted process, we bounce back and forth between wanting the painful or unwanted elements to end and being willing to tolerate them. In the midst of this process, we may even find ourselves becoming interested in this experience of being in conflict, and instead of wanting to get rid of it, we want it to hang on long enough to reveal to us what is really going on. We may then find that we have transitioned into a receptive or explorative process.

I believe that when the conflicted process is banished from the meditative process, our whole meditation practice suffers from the loss and becomes inauthentic. Most meditation techniques either deny that such a conflicted process exists or have strategies in place to curb its impact and control its course. Practices denying the existence of conflict are often those that present meditation as only peaceful, relaxing, and eventually transcendent. Being in conflict, especially about the technique you are doing, is not part of the deal. Even experiencing emotional conflicts around difficult decisions, painful memories, or uncertain future plans may be perceived as taking you away from the true way of meditating.

Practices that tend to curb the conflicted process and lead it toward a good, wholesome outcome are much more subtly aversive to conflict, but still so. For instance, the instruction to accept whatever you experience with equanimity appears on the surface to suggest that you accept all of your experiences no matter what they are, but underneath there's a message that says, "Don't react to it." So you end up not accepting your reactions because you're not supposed to have any.

Other Conflicted Areas

The conflicted process is not just about the struggle caused by trying to do a generative practice when the conditions are not right for it. It goes much deeper and is much more extensive than that, for there is more to a meditation practice than just the instructions. You can be in conflict over the instructions and attempt to subdue your conflict regarding "doubt," and in the process, still continue to experience the conflict as the unacknowledged background of your practice. Such conflict regarding the beliefs and views you're taught, and consequently are supposed to embody or realize, is not something to be banished but something to bring into your practice. To sit with how you disagree with a particular teaching, and learn to become aware of both the articulation of beliefs within the teaching and the views you hold that are contrary to those beliefs, is a way to use the conflicted process rather than avoid it.

In a similar vein, conflicts over morals, ethics, or any rules and standards of behavior found within your practice will arise and will require attention, not just surrender. When we too easily adopt a foreign standard of behavior, one that comes from a culture that is not our own and of which we know little, we tend to give it far greater importance and significance than the ethics and morals we grew up with. The Buddhist monastic codes and the way Western monks tend to worship them and follow them unquestioningly is a perfect example of this. Many Western monks and nuns try to obey the rules as best they can, even though some of the rules do not make sense from the point of view of the culture they come from. Rebelling against the rules is really not possible in a monastic community where everyone not only adheres to them but also sees them as an integral part of the path toward liberation of mind.

Lay Buddhist practitioners also experience conflict with the rules of conduct they must obey while on retreat or decide to take into their daily lives and can become even more self-conscious and self-critical than before. Instead of reflecting on these new codes of behavior and staying with the internal struggles they naturally bring, some people simply force themselves to obey the new rules. And this may not be limited just to forcing upon themselves the new rules of conduct but may even extend to restrictions on how they think and feel. Some people may come to believe they should never feel their anger or listen to their cravings, as if our emotions could obey a decision not to feel compelled to act on them. Some may even go so far as to believe that adherence to this new code of behavior will enable them to no longer feel the undesirable feelings. The practice becomes not about cultivating beneficial qualities but about suppressing unwanted behaviors, controlling thoughts and feelings, and acting in ways that can at times be false and misleading.

But if, once you've taken up the new code of behavior, you allow the conflicts with it to emerge, then there can be a healthy tension between the newly adopted code of conduct and your accustomed behaviors. Take for instance someone who has taken up the precept not to speak ill of others (a part of right speech). This precept makes good sense and, if followed, will lead not only to less guilt over what one says but also to fewer conflicts with others. But what if someone is accustomed to criticizing corrupt and dangerous politicians, arrogant and autocratic bosses, or people who lack scruples? These acts of speech seem normal and even necessary at times. They're easily justified. Adhering to the precept of not speaking ill of others can be very difficult in these situations. When you do speak ill of another, you might feel guilty and self-critical because of your efforts to follow the precept, and you may then vow never to do it again, which, of course, just leads to more guilt and self-hatred when you end up doing it again. In this way, the conflict becomes about your failure to keep the precept, which is not where learning about the conflict takes place.

The learning is found in recognizing when the new mode of conduct (not speaking ill of others) and the preexisting behavior (self-justified criticism of others) rub up against each other, pulling you in both directions. So in this situation, you may take up the intention to train yourself not to speak ill of others instead of taking up a rule not to do so. You may be willing to learn how to move from being critical of others to greater acceptance and understanding of them as they are. In that process, there will be many failures, though each failure can be an opportunity to learn what makes it hard for you to tolerate certain people and to observe your unwillingness to look into the causes and conditions for the way they are and the feelings they stir up in you.

The conflicted process challenges us in so many ways, how can it not be a part of the path for each of us, especially in meditation, where conflicts are bound to emerge just by the fact that we are with our minds for the duration of each sitting? It seems to be the case that just about every meditation sitting, at least for most beginners, begins with the conflicted process. This brings us to another element of my theory, which I call the primary transition.

18

The Primary Transition

Every time you begin a meditation sitting, whether you're a beginner or a longtime practitioner, you go through a transition from your states of mind preceding the meditation sitting to those that will arise within the sitting. During this primary transition, any one of the three basic meditative processes (receptive, generative, or conflicted) will usually be operating.

In mainstream meditation practices this transition is generally considered either as a period to prepare the mind for meditation or as something to be gotten through as soon as possible. For instance, Vipassana students are often instructed to begin a meditation sitting by immediately putting their attention on the breath at the nostrils or the abdomen and to continually return the attention there when the mind wanders from it. Or a student may be given a series of rituals to put herself in the right frame of mind for meditation, some phrases to repeat, some vows to recite, or objects to contemplate or visualize at the outset of a sitting.

This common way of beginning is not a smooth or gradual transition that incorporates what went on before but a harsh break from your previous state. The transitional aspect of this change from one activity to another is not usually given significance. Instead, all of your attention is focused on what you need to do as you start meditating, and whatever was happening before is intentionally let go of rather than transitioned out of.

Launching into a meditation sitting with complete disregard for what you're bringing into it creates an artificial division between your mental processes outside of meditation and what they should be like in meditation. It sets up and supports the notion that your mind should behave differently in meditation, or be of another order, such as perfectly aware and calm. This kind of division contributes to the struggle, frustration, and conflict that occurs in meditation sittings.

When doing a generative practice, often at the beginning of a sitting, you're drawn into the conflicted process. You try to get your mind to quiet down and focus on the object of meditation. The transition at the beginning of the sitting could then have a flavor of trying to tame your mind, slow it down, and get it to stay put. If that finally happens, the transition is over, and you might feel that now you're finally meditating. If that doesn't happen, then what you expected to be just a transitory conflict lasts much of the sitting.

People do have meditation sittings where they do a generative practice and there is little or no struggle with their mind at the outset. The transition between where they were before meditation and during the sitting is then usually very short. If the practice is observing the breath, then awareness of the breath is easy to maintain. If *metta,* the feelings and sensations come readily, and so on. But even if the conflicted process has been averted, it still does not go away, as something can easily happen within the sitting to upset your calm or concentration. After recovering from such an interruption of concentration, it may feel as though you are beginning the sitting all over again and that you have to find a way to transition back into a calm state of mind.

This brings up the whole notion of transitions in a meditation sitting. How many are there? There can be several in a single sitting. In fact, there can be many periods you'd like to transition out of in a given sitting, as well as periods where a pleasant state of mind emerges that you'd like to transition into more fully. These are secondary transitions, occurring within the context of having already made the initial transition into the meditation sitting.

The Primary Transition with the Receptive Process

When you begin a meditation sitting with the receptive process, the state of mind you're in as you enter the sitting affects how the sitting will unfold. There is no line marking the end of what was on your mind before you sat and what develops as you sit. Such transitions do not always follow the same pattern, and you may feel very little has shifted far into the sitting, or you might experience some dramatic shifts toward the beginning, or anything in between.

I will go into some examples of primary transitions, starting with a meditation journal I received from someone whom I never met. This individual heard about me from a colleague and contacted me. I asked him to journal a series of meditation sittings and then set up a time to talk on the phone. The way he goes through the primary transition, highlighted in italic type, has some features that will be recognizable to anyone who is becoming receptive to the primary transition.

First sitting: *Much body restlessness (five to ten minutes) with temptation to go to breath to settle down. Images appear, with noise in the background—muffled sound/word. No clear verbal thinking. Images appear disjointed—images from the day are most prominent. Difficult to recall. There appears to be no focus. Then anxiety appears in the form of chest tightness. A vivid thought occurs: "What if someone breaks in?"* Then sleep comes—I estimate two to five minutes of drowsiness. This happens two or three times during the sitting. As this happens, and each time it does, I am suddenly jolted from sleep by a vivid sensation that I am choking and unable to breathe. Every time

this happens, I am jolted awake. It is very unpleasant to experience this. At twenty to the hour high alertness occurs—
very awake. The images decrease and there are episodes of
stillness. Several thoughts enter: "Is this really meditation?"
Gradually nausea sets in. A headache, eye ache, and lower
back pain join in. I feel I will vomit. By the one-hour mark
I stop. Interestingly, so does the nausea and body ache.

Second sitting: *Begin with intense anxiety arising in chest,
stomach. With hypersalivation. Thinking occurs—difficult to describe, as they are not entirely verbal, but they imply a profound
sense of inadequacy, and this ties into anxiety about going to work
tomorrow. The thoughts imply that somehow I will be perceived as
inadequate, not good enough and inferior by coworkers at my company. This is accompanied by random, neutral images of the work
setting. Wander into other thoughts (don't remember them). When
I realize that this has happened, I also notice that the anxiety is
gone.* Anxiety goes up and down after this—fluctuates (gently). Interestingly, I notice that the images that accompany
the anxiety appear entirely unrelated and are in fact quite
pleasant. They are images of a painting, of flowers, grass,
then a field emerging. Thought occurs about meditation—
I feel defeated—there are endless layers to the mind: "How
will I ever make any sense of it or what do I do about it?"
"What do I focus on?" Things settle and the images continue. Physical anxiety abates.

If there is no line dividing the beginning of the meditation sitting
from the rest of it, how can I mark the end of a transition in these
meditation sittings? Instead of a line marking the end of the transition, it might be more accurate to say that there is a transitional period of experience that occurs, after which the meditator feels more
inside the meditation. This period of experience occurs on account
of the segment of experience that began the meditation sitting sub-
siding completely or moving out of the foreground.

The initial segment of experience in the second meditation
sitting above:

Begin with intense anxiety arising in chest, stomach. With hypersalivation. Thinking occurs—difficult to describe, as they are not entirely verbal, but they imply a profound sense of inadequacy, and this ties into anxiety about going to work tomorrow. The thoughts imply that somehow I will be perceived as inadequate, not good enough and inferior by coworkers at my company.

The transitional period of experience:

> This is accompanied by random, neutral images of the work setting. Wander into other thoughts (don't remember them). When I realize that this has happened, I also notice that the anxiety is gone.

What distinguishes the initial segment of experience from the transitional period is that it is coherently related to things on the person's mind before the sitting began. It is a carryover of what he was feeling or thinking about before he sat down. The transitional period of experience, however, usually has elements that are not carryovers from what was occupying the person's attention before the sitting. The meditator's mind is acting differently. Thoughts and images may lose their coherence and thus be experienced as more random and less embedded in a narrative. This, of course, is frequently experienced when entering a pre-*jhanic* (or hypnagogic) state but is not limited to that kind of transition. An important feature of the transition is that something that was in the foreground of your experience at the beginning, such as anxiety, moves into the background or vanishes altogether.

Here is another example, from a man who has attended some of my workshops and retreats.

> At the start of the sit (and for about half an hour prior to it) I was noticing lustful thoughts. It felt like my attention and focus were being pulled outside myself toward half-formed nonverbal images and memories, mostly recent ones from

the hour before—the sensation of being "pulled" was very tangible. Simultaneously I noticed (and preferred to notice) my body, visual field, and thoughts settling down, and a mildly buzzing descending tingling start on the surface of my skin and just under it. I was interested to watch the lustful thoughts and erotic images, but they didn't progress much and faded after about five minutes, which surprised me, since they had seemed to have such energy.

The rest of the sit alternated between brief episodes of random content-laden thought about the odds and ends of daily life, punctuated by longer episodes of quiet spatial blankness. The blankness seemed to have a lot of depth to it, and I mostly focused on this and the dark and static, but not completely uniform, visual field. These reminded me of quiet sits on retreat where there was nothing but a very big dark space with a vague area of focus on it and, in the background, an acknowledgment of watching it. I frequently drooped during these episodes, and they typically ended when I straightened myself up. Toward the end of the sit, I decided not to bother straightening. Three or four times faintly luminous amorphous images started forming and dancing in the blank visual field—I found this interesting but didn't do much to sustain it. Several times I noticed a contented happiness and automatically checked to see if it was correlated with tingling, but it seemed very disconnected from the tingling, which was mild and didn't attract much attention the few times I was aware of it. I also remember occasionally hearing external sounds (the doorbell upstairs, water moving through pipes, the sprinklers outside), and my body felt cold. When the bell rang, I was surprised how quickly the time had passed.

The primary transition in this meditation sitting was taken up with lustful thoughts. In the first few minutes, the meditator became aware of his attention being pulled toward half-formed images and memories from an hour before the sitting began. Then he describes simultaneously noticing his body, his (internal) visual field, his thoughts settling down, and tingling along his skin. It is here that he is making a transition. A notable feature of this kind of transition, found in the previous person's sittings as well, is that the mind becomes more diffuse, less focused on one thing in particular. It is thus no surprise that the lustful thoughts and images lose their energy, as they no longer occupy the meditator's central focus, dissipated by an awareness that is able to include more aspects of his experience than before. The rest of the meditation sitting progresses in a peaceful, contented manner, resembling what, from the outside, would be a relaxing and refreshing meditation sitting.

Allowing our sittings to begin with the receptive process is also a way to surrender control over the course and direction of them. Contrary to what is commonly believed, being receptive to what comes up at the beginning of a meditation sitting can lead to transitioning into calm, settled, and aware states. It can also facilitate the emergence of the three developed meditative processes (explorative, non–taking up, and connected).

19

Unlearning Meditation and the Generative Process

Many of the reservations people have about unlearning meditation relate to the value and usefulness of generative practices. I tend to paint a negative picture of such practices, focusing more on their problems instead of their benefits. But that is because I actually see that generative practices are best used when you're in the generative process. When you're in a conflicted process, where there is a struggle to do the instructions, that's not the right time to use a generative practice. When you're in a receptive process and less able to hold your attention on a single object, then it will also be difficult to do any of the generative practices that require a strong focus. But when you are truly able to hold your attention on an object of meditation and do a generative instruction without effort, that is the right time to do such a practice.

You might think that what I am describing here is an ideal scenario and one that doesn't happen all that often. But actually it happens quite frequently. We find ourselves able to do a meditation practice that we have tried to do "with effort" and have previously failed at. By associating generation with effort in meditation, we miss the fact that our minds are quite capable of focusing, creating, and learning without being forced to do so. Our minds are naturally generative.

What we are unlearning in meditation is the notion that we should be doing generative practices all the time, and with great effort, in order to attain their benefits. We are not unlearning the generative practices themselves—I never recommend that students stop doing traditional practices that have been helpful to them. I just suggest that they come to a place in their sittings where such practices begin to arise more receptively, and then they can apply added attention to those generated objects of meditation in order to go deeper into the generative practice they are accustomed to doing. The only time I would tell a student to reconsider doing a generative practice is when it has become automatic, forced, or in some way detrimental to the person's psyche.

Although I don't teach generative practices—you will never find me leading a guided meditation—I do suggest that students become aware when the conditions appear to be right to do a particular practice they have confidence in.

I recently co-led a workshop with Ken McLeod, a teacher in the Tibetan tradition, in which we traded off teaching one-hour segments throughout the day. The initial periods of meditation were instructed as found in this book, while the last meditation of the day was a guided meditation led by Ken. He began with directing students' attention to bodily and sense experience, then gradually expanding it to mental and emotional experience, and from there to specific aspects of the mind, and finally he gave instructions to generate wholesome states of mind. Many of the people found the guided meditation easy to do and that it led them into new experiences and insights. Some people could not follow the guided meditation at certain intervals and so sat with what came up for them.

For the people who found this easy, it was an example of doing a generative practice within an existing generative process. I believe that some of the reason they found it easy to do was that they had been sitting in a more receptive mode earlier in the day. The receptive process, especially when it leads to periods of exploration, tends to clear away the impediments to doing generative practices. Many students have remarked to me how when they have switched from sitting receptively to doing a particular structured meditation practice, the practice can be accomplished with greater ease and less effort than usual.

The transition from a receptive process to a generative one can be smooth, though you may soon become aware of the change of effort in the sitting. When you're receptive, experiences just come to you without any willing involved, and you can get quite comfortable with that and view it as the norm. So when you shift into a generative process receptively, it may take some recalibration regarding how much effort to apply. Often people don't apply enough effort and therefore miss out on an opportunity to use the generative productively and skillfully. Other times they apply a strong intention and approach the experience with too much force and so need to readjust their effort in order to use the generative process.

> Quiet seems very loud and I listen to the quiet, which translates into the *Om* sound. Then I notice how much effort I am making to make the sound of silence into the *Om* sound, so I relax the effort.

There can also be a sense of clinging to experiences, or elaborating upon them, when you move into a generative process, and many meditators tend to be warned against this when they are practicing in a tradition that values "letting go." You might think that I support "letting go" at those times, but I don't generally. I see clinging to experiences and elaborating on them, or thinking about them, as being quite natural and nothing to be alarmed about. When someone makes a huge story about an experience in meditation while it is going on, it is all right to allow the story to go on until it reaches a place where a transition to something else occurs. Then reflecting back on the story can provide some insight as to what kept it alive.

I have heard many reports of meditation sittings where someone has written an article, composed a piece of music, planned an

art project, or redecorated her house, and it was actually very productive and efficient to be doing this in meditation. Such events
are also instances of the generative process, though there seems
to be no meditation practice associated with this kind of creative
process, quite understandably. But since it is happening in a meditation sitting, it is meditative, and the mind is using the qualities it
has developed in meditation to accomplish this particular mental
task.

We are often warned against using meditation to work on a
project, we should drop those thoughts and get back to sitting
with awareness. But when the generative process is active, it is
not easy to get back to a receptive process (or even to generate
something other than what holds our interest). There is often a
momentum pushing the whole project along, and one can only
surrender to it or fight it. By surrendering to it, you'll go through
the thoughts on the project, occasionally feeding them, until there
is some gradual dissipation of the energy behind the thoughts.
This is being receptive with the generative process, allowing it to
flourish, knowing that at some point you will inevitably transition
into another process.

20

The Three Developed Meditative Processes

The three developed meditative processes are the explorative, the non–taking up, and the connected. They are ways our mind has learned to relate to experiences through meditation, and they are not meant to be taken as optimal meditative experiences. In fact, this theory of the meditative process does not attempt to go beyond what people would ordinarily experience in meditation and so makes no conjectures as to what an awakened or enlightened consciousness is.

The Explorative Process

The explorative process may initially appear as discursive thought about your experience. Meditation practices that do not value thinking will often disregard this aspect of the budding explorative process. I often have to ask several questions about the nature of a student's internal dialogues in meditation for the student to pick up on the explorative nature of his or her discursive thinking. When you're having an internal dialogue (or monologue) about what is going on in your sitting or about the subject of meditation or on a concept about your experience, it is likely that there is an explorative process occurring.

How can you tell? First of all, the explorations are open-ended. There isn't much of a drive to find an answer, reach a conclusion, arrive at completion. You're engaged in the process of exploration without the need to wrap it up too quickly or too neatly with a good idea, though such ideas might occur and move the exploration along in interesting directions, as in this person's sitting.

> Sitting in a state of agitation because I had to wake a neighbor up to get him to move his car so my wife could leave for work. That agitated state continued into the meditation sitting. I'm appreciating my time at the Zen center because I really was removed from a lot of the world that disturbs me now. I'm concerned about the political situation, and my anxiety comes up. Or does my anxiety express itself in those thoughts? Tightness around my solar plexus. Internal dialogues followed where I was being right, winning the argument. Comforting myself, my survival assured. Reflected for a while on my relentless desire to be. Being is satisfying and fear of loss of being creates anxiety. The double-edged sword of Manjusri. Noticing how a thought or feeling can branch out in all directions.

Then there is how the explorative process is an outgrowth of the receptive process. One is led along in the exploration. There seems to be less self-agency in it along with a willingness to go into painful or difficult areas that you would normally avoid. It can have the feel of going back and forth from staying with an experience (an emotion, a train of thought, a sensation, or any combination thereof) and observing it. You can test your observations by bringing your attention back to the experience (either remembered or, if it is still accessible, in the present) and seeing whether the concepts actually line up with it. There are no perfect examples of this process, as it is not a technique to be done but, rather, a diffuse and disorganized process one is led through, as in this journal entry.

This sitting was especially hard to get a grip on afterward—at first seemed almost impossible to recall anything, like a deep dream that's slipped away. Most noticeable episode was when I had been sitting for about fifteen minutes with a sort of tension in upper chest and shoulder area. It was associated with an unpleasant feeling and thoughts that were vague and not really noticed.

Very fleeting image of a sort of plane of light or light color extending away from my body to the right side, and with it a kind of sliding movement. It became like an exit of some sort, and the tension slid away as if someone had opened a doorway onto an expansive place.

When the tension around it was removed (or rather not being maintained) and the physical sensation of tension and hunching over in a protective posture were seen clearly and also eased, it became evident that "inside" was an unpleasant feeling that was subtle but almost unbearable when I really registered it. It was kind of exquisite but awful—felt inescapable, like it was part of everything, had no edges or limits. I think that's why it was so hard to bear. I noticed it and then there was a kind of quiet panic, like I couldn't open to it for very long. Then it changed and I can't remember what happened. I think I moved my attention elsewhere. Even so, at the end of the sitting there was a mixed feeling of fear of the boundless unpleasantness, marked vulnerability, and a kind of relief (from having connected with it).

Often there is a degree of *samadhi* in the explorative process, where you're tranquil as your mind goes through some difficult feelings or memories and begins to pick up things about them. Some of these sittings, like the one above, can have periods that are hard to recollect, but when going through them, you may be fairly aware of the thoughts, feelings, observations, and the way of knowing your experience. Even if very little is recalled, such experiences of exploration within a *samadhi* state have a characteristic sense of your having gotten to something very deep and hidden about yourself.

The painful feeling the meditator connected with in the sitting above had many dimensions to it as she stayed with it and explored it. Her names for it and ideas about it emerged from her exploration of it. At the time, there was little if any interpretation of this subtle unpleasant feeling, though after the sitting she did interpret the experience in her journal: "Afterward I reflected that painting brings me in touch with this exposed, vulnerable feeling, because there is no edge to it, it can't ever be perfected or finished. This has been on my mind because I've been painting every day this week." It is common to come up with some kind of meaning for such experiences afterward, because we do need our explorations to provide us with something we can use in our lives. Instead of trying to stop interpreting experiences, we can become aware of the effect these interpretations have on us, how we use them, and why we believe them.

Going Further into the Explorative Process

To further illustrate the explorative process, I am going to look at a series of journal entries by one individual. Her name is Joan, and she has been a student of mine for about four years. She has been meditating for about thirty years and was practicing Vipassana meditation before she met me. At the time she met me, she would primarily let her attention go to sounds when she meditated. She would also, rarely, focus on the breath, and she would occasionally do *metta* practice. Even though she had also done "choiceless awareness" meditation practice at some point in her past, she hadn't really allowed thoughts and feelings to carry her along in her sittings until she sat a ten-day retreat with me. Since then, she has loosened up considerably in her meditation practice and has become comfortable with this way of meditating for most of her sittings.

These journal entries demonstrate several aspects of the explorative process, including what has already been said. One important aspect is how we pick up certain areas of exploration and stay with them for a period of time, which is why a series of journal entries is so helpful. A particular area will have a hold on us—we are very interested in it at that time.

Another side to the explorative process is the exploration of the practice you're doing. Since these journal entries are from someone who has been meditating with the Recollective Awareness approach for a few years, there is less doubting of this practice in her contemplations on it and more investigating the value of it. Still, key elements of it are subject to scrutiny.

There are also several explorations concerning the nature of how we know our experience. Putting our attention on the ways we know what is happening (the process) is much different from what it is we know (the content). We can know, for instance, that we are hearing a particular sound and what that sound is. That is knowing the content of our experience. We may also know that the sound comes and goes, that it arises and passes away due to conditions. That is knowing the process of our experience. But that is just the beginning of our exploration into the various ways of knowing our experience.

> This sit was interesting in that it took a different point of interest halfway through. I had a few things on my mind before the sit . . . and they all arose in various forms and to various degrees in the transition period . . . the tennis I had just been watching, the letter to a friend who has cancer, the email to another friend . . . my father's wife, school, a meeting I recently attended. They all sort of arose and sank, arose and sank, in waves of different intensity and clarity. There was a sense of the awareness of this arising and falling. Then a sense of the awareness of that. Then a kind of big picturing of it all . . . a broadened awareness of all that was being experienced. It seemed like all at once but it probably had varying degrees of a major/minor focus if I really go back to recall.
>
> It felt like an awareness of all the sense-doors experience. These sensations were the whole catastrophe of what I was picking up. There was a ringing sound of tinnitus, with a

background sound of the sea and the sound of my husband walking around . . . all with apparently equal pick-up value.

Then a taste in the mouth, sensations in the body, belly, legs, face, a background image of the body being there and a kind of tone of awareness of it all, even the colors on the eyes.

There was an easiness, a resting in the "big picture," but also awareness of the movement toward and away from this. Like when it all stopped being equal and a dominance oc- curred or a preference, then the movement would go to- ward personalizing it all . . . a story, a sense of my face . . . a hook into a fantasy, a carrying on of what would otherwise have been just there. So really there was an awareness of the movement in and out (wavelike again), of taking what was arising as personal . . . or broad focus to specific focus . . . in and out again . . . in and out. Then there would be a jolt of realization that something would have been taken so personally that big-picture awareness was gone and I was absorbed in the story line again . . . then outward the focus would go to breath and impartiality again.

This description gives a feel for how Vipassana meditation sit- tings are generally talked about, with references to "arising and falling," "witnessing and personalizing," and "broad and specific focus." Most notably there is this experience: "There was a sense of the awareness of this arising and falling. Then a sense of the awareness of that. Then a kind of big picturing of it all . . . a broad- ened awareness of all that was being experienced." In later journal entries, Joan makes attempts to assure me that this is not a concept but a real experience.

What is her experience of being aware of her awareness of aris- ing and falling? "It felt like an awareness of all the sense-doors ex- perience. These sensations were the whole catastrophe of what I was picking up . . . all with apparent equal pick-up value." Her way of knowing tastes, sensations, images, colors, and her body sitting was such that each sense impression was somehow equal, there being no dominance of one over another or preference for one over another. When the "pick up" stopped being equal it was because she found herself in a story or hooked into a fantasy, where experiences were once again taken personally. She was aware of going in and out of this way of knowing her experiences as being equal, seeing it as moving from the "big picture" to being "absorbed in the story line."

The exploration initiated in this sitting continues in future sittings, as in this one six weeks later.

There was a sense of being with whatever hit my senses, but it was almost overlaid with a question that started as just a focused curiosity that soon became an actual question. It was something like "What's the difference between how this is being picked up now and what would be picked up if there were no craving/aversion? What's the difference between this mind and a liberated mind?"

I tried to pick up a quality about it that would show the difference. Would even the curiosity about the difference be a form of craving? Where was the subtle sense of judgment that would make that difference? Was it the sense of there being an "I" who was picking it up? I kind of played around with these questions and the sense of there being some karma formed with the process. I could go into the quality of it but always inevitably zoomed out to the one watching it and therefore commentating. Whatever was happening, the transitions felt smooth and free-flowing.

Then I went into a time of thinking about *metta*. I'm not sure if I thought of my friend who has cancer first, or the idea of *metta* practice first, but I went over a few scenarios of what is happening to him in his life and then went into an old practice of visualizing him and sending him love through the out-breath. It actually moved into imagining his body with cancer in it, almost like sooty deposits through his veins/organs, and on each out-breath pushing it out, like dust moving out through his skin pores.

I did this for quite a while. On occasion going back to when I was a student and doing a similar practice (predharma days) in trying to use strength of mind to send an image to a friend. I could remember the bed I was in and the sense of focus I had while doing it. It was a strong visual memory. This turned into a sidetrack again. Interested in how memory was working with this. It was almost not recalled but "dropped in" due to the familiarity with the same sense of the power of visualization.

This is almost becoming an area of interest in my sits now. How recall works and the different types of recall and different levels of agency involved. Sometimes I just can't see the process and sometimes the decision is obvious.

This time the sitting starts with an explorative process. Joan is receptively aware of whatever is "hitting" her senses, while curiosity forms into a question around picking up sense impressions with a mind that has craving and aversion in it and one that does not. She reports this exploration as being overlaid onto her experience of being aware of the sense doors, but it doesn't seem to be affecting it as the story lines did in the sitting six weeks prior. She is wondering about self and karma in the experience, and she "could go into the quality of it but always inevitably zoomed out to the one watching it and therefore commentating." I surmise that she was going back and forth between what she directly sensed and her exploration of it, which contained observations and ideas on the experience.

After that she moves into the generative process when she remembers a friend's illness. She does a *metta* practice for him for a while. It seems perfectly natural for her to do this, and she reflects on the habits she has formed in meditation in regard to *metta* practice. But from going into the memories of this practice, she then emerges once again into an exploration of memory. This is not because she wants to explore the subject of memory as a topic to pursue but because of an experience that confronts her notions about it. She wrote, "It was almost not recalled but 'dropped in' due to the familiarity with the same sense of the power of visualization." This sets the stage for the area of exploration found in another sitting a month later.

On shutting my eyes, I sank really quickly into "just listening" as sounds arose. There was very little energy. I was just taking it in. A sort of interest in it arose. Then the recalling process came into interest. It occurred to me that "being with" something involved a recalling process of just a few seconds. It was like a net being cast back. In being aware of what was happening now—like sounds and sensations— the net was just cast back a nanosecond. At other times the net was cast a little further back. Then on that jolt of "Where was I?" cast back quickly for the past few incidents. I watched this for a while. The image was not so much a net but a sort of amoebic foot that would stretch back, bringing experience to mind in a constant process of recall. It could be broad or thin, specific or general, deliberate or automatic. It seemed like the recall process was the whole of awareness. One of the benefits of Recollective Awareness! With the sense of noticing comes the awareness of context and what brings it on. And then there is taking it less personally.

The meditation sitting begins with her entering a process where she could just listen to the sounds around her and take them in. An interest in the sounds arises, but soon after, she becomes interested in the recalling process. She sees that "being with" an experience is not in the present moment, as she had been taught, but rather involves a recollection of an experience. She has discovered a fact of her experience that directly contradicts the view of mindfulness as being only in the present moment. If awareness is always after the fact, then any moment when you become aware of something, you're actually calling that back to mind. When she has the experience of wondering where she has been in the sitting, she can recall a series of events that occurred. This exploration provides an understanding of how her mind works in meditation when becoming aware of things, which does not fit in with the conceptual model of experience that she previously believed in. She finds exploring the operations of awareness engaging, and she continues to discover new things about it. For instance, she sees that by recollecting experiences in this way, she can better see the context and how these things came to be. In that process, she learns that she is taking things less personally.

The Explorative Process and Transformative Conceptualization

Much of the work that is done to go beyond concepts in the transformative conceptualization process occurs in the explorative process. You could rightly say that transformative conceptualization is a type of exploration, but it's not the only kind of exploration that can occur. It is also the outcome of a series of explorations, which, while one is in them, may give no indication that your perception of things will be diminished or abandoned by the process of exploring them. The third step of the transformative conceptualization process that I outlined in chapter 12 may just come about without any warning or any intention.

In the meditation Joan had on the day following the previous meditation sitting, she stumbled upon this third step.

My mind went over a few things from the day but quickly went into watching the recall process. I actually now see it as a "thinking-through-concepts process" scattered amongst watching the "thinking-through process" and watching the "being-with" process. Hard to pinpoint and explain.

Joan notices three separate processes: (1) the "thinking-through-concepts process," (2) watching the "thinking-through process," and (3) watching the "being with" process. The thinking-through-concepts process describes investigative thinking that uses concepts we have already learned. In some cases, it might involve investigating whether the definition of a word actually fits the experience we are having. In other cases it might be how a particular concept, such as "the now," applies to what we're experiencing. These are the first two steps in the transformative conceptualization process, of naming an experience and moving to a new description of it.

When she watches "thinking-through," she notices the thinking-through-concepts process she is engaged in. She is not exclusively thinking things through but also witnessing that process. In this way the concepts she arrives at through thinking in the meditation get looked at as part of the thinking process. When this happens she begins to see how concepts function and thus begins to treat them less as ideas to be held on to and believed in for all time and more as related to a particular effect of a moment of understanding about her experience. Then the concept, label, or interpretation has done its job and can be dropped. This is the third step of seeing into the narrative of the experience.

> I was revisiting in thought my previous thinking that one can't "be in the moment" because that nanosecond of experience makes no sense if its not in context. I went through this in my mind trying to articulate it . . . or trying to actually test it and experience it . . . then articulate it. Any of the so-called being in the now involves recall, even if to the minutest degree, because without a "being in context" the nanoseconds of experience wouldn't make sense.

Here Joan drops the concept she learned at the beginning of her meditation practice, the notion of being in the now. It makes no sense to her. In the explorative process, as she tries to articulate it to herself in the sitting, she tests it against her experience. It no longer makes sense because she is seeing it in relation to another concept, based on her experience, that all experiences arise within a context: experiences cannot be singled out from the conditions out of which they arise, such as the preceding moment, and thus there cannot be a present moment without a past moment.

This may sound like an intellectual process, because it deals with concepts, but in meditation sittings, it is an experiential process of exploring the function of concepts. In this series of sittings, Joan has looked into her experiences of being aware and has seen that the most pragmatic approach is to define awareness as recollection rather than as present-moment awareness or mindfulness. It is through explorations such as this that you can feel confident in dropping a concept that the larger meditation community has generally taken as being true and valid.

21

The Non–Taking-Up Process

At first hearing, the term *non–taking up* may sound awkward. It is not as clear as words and phrases with similar meanings, such as *nonattachment* or *nongrasping*. Why would I choose to use this awkward expression instead of these others? First of all, "taking up" is different from attachment or grasping. With attachment we have a notion of two things being joined, of their clinging to each other, or in a psychological sense, of an unhealthy way of holding on to people and things. The word *grasping* has a similar sense, though it perhaps carries greater force, especially when it is taken as "holding tightly." *Taking up* includes the capacity of choice within the process of holding on to something and therefore does not have the feel of being an impersonal, strictly determined habit. There is more freedom in the taking up of something than there is in being attached to something or grasping it.

What do I really mean by *taking up* in regard to meditation? I mean several things:

- Choosing to hold on to experiences
- Intentionally building upon or fueling an experience

- Believing in the self-structure that has formed around an experience

I will now go into the following three areas in relation to the non–taking-up process.

- Where there are no choices to hold on to experiences
- No intentional building or fueling of experiences
- No beliefs in the self-structures that form around our experiences

Where There Are No Choices to Hold On to Experiences

This is the most basic form of non–taking up (or "not taking up," whichever sounds better to you) and can be arrived at through a variety of practices, not just the approach I teach. In a general but imprecise sense, it may be likened to a flow experience of "arising and passing away" in Vipassana meditation. Nothing is held on to in one's experience for any significant duration. Thoughts tend to vanish immediately upon being noticed, feelings arise for an instant and gently subside, and bodily sensations are generally pleasant and transitory. Not only is there a flow to the rapidly changing experiences, but there seems to be less volition in the process. Things are happening on their own; choices are not arising. Most particularly, choices to hold on to a particular experience rarely surface except, of course, when the flowing stops and everything slows down and becomes more "normal" once again. Then choices to hold on to or get rid of certain experiences appear more often.

The non–taking-up process grows out of tolerating the intensity and duration of your meditation experiences. When we become more able to tolerate intense, painful, and/or long-lasting experiences, we find that we hold on to them less and less. It is often the case that people have flow experiences following upon periods of tolerating discomfort, agitation, and intense emotions. There are even a few longtime meditators who regularly meditate for long periods and endure all kinds of physical pain in order to arrive at the non–taking-up process.

A key feature of meditation practices in which you sit motionless through intense pain (which I would caution against) is that the choice to move is constantly dismissed. Other choices to do things in the meditation are also summarily disregarded. So it seems to me that such practices serve to reduce the power of choices that arise in your sittings, though they do so in favor of following one strict line of direction: to sit through the pain.

Now, of course, people will also arrive at the non–taking-up process, or at least this form of it, through meditation practices that are essentially painless and calming. Choiceless awareness practice, for example, often leads to these experiences of "arising and passing away," which happens by not trying to hold attention on anything for too long. Instead, the meditator lets his attention go from one object to another, not making choices beforehand, allowing the attention to go where it will for a moment before moving on.

Other Vipassana practices, such as body scanning (S. N. Goenka's method) and noting the body and sense doors (the Mahasi Sayadaw method), also lead to the non–taking-up process. Body scanning, or "sweeping," is a practice where the meditator moves one's attention up and down the body. The technique starts slowly and carefully, but after a few days spent doing this practice on retreat, the speed and ease of doing it can increase dramatically. The moving of one's attention up and down one's body and limbs can be highly focusing, and combined with the increased tolerance for painful sensations, it often leads to a non–taking-up process. Though often described at Goenka's retreats as a free-flow experience, it is technically considered to be of the nature of a rapid arising-and-passing-away experience. Arriving at this state of mind is one of the objectives of that meditation practice and would be considered an optimal experience, though it is still not seen as the final goal.

The noting practice of the Mahasi method, in which the meditator notes each moment of experience with a label, also leads to the non–taking-up process, though the experiences are of a different sort than those experienced in body-scanning practice. Noting your experience as it is happening has a way of concentrating the mind on discrete, separate moments of experience. It breaks the habitual mode of perceiving thoughts, feelings, and sensations as having a duration in time. Instead, what would normally be considered a painful sensation, such as a dull lower back pain, would not be looked at as a continuous sensation but as made up of moments that follow linearly, one ending before the other begins, having no connection with each other. The fact that the person just keeps noting "pain," "pain," several times a minute breaks up the notion of there being a continuous sensation.

I would say that this noting practice does create greater tolerance for the painful experience while at the same time turning it into something impersonal. That it eventually leads to a non–taking-up process is no surprise. As in the Goenka method, the non–taking-up process is not the final goal, though it is still considered an optimal state and may even be found as the basis for the definition of *equanimity* as taught in that tradition.

No Intentional Building or Fueling of Experiences

The meditation practices described in the last section can also lead to not building upon experiences, but they do it by *not* having the student look at the building process. In unlearning meditation, you concentrate on the ways experiences build and form, exploring them while trying to understand their dependently arisen nature. In this way, non–taking up is a state of mind that arises out of the explorative process. It is *not* arrived at through techniques of focusing your attention on prescribed objects of meditation or by breaking experiences down into discrete moments or separate parts. It is arrived at through staying with and tolerating the ways we fuel our experiences and through investigating that process.

It may appear to be a contradiction that by allowing ourselves to receptively go into our experiences and let them flourish we will not take them up and build upon them. Through a series of processes (usually receptive and explorative), you can begin to disentangle from building upon experiences and eventually begin not taking them up. This is a way of arriving at "letting go" by gradually loosening your hold. And that is how it often feels to people—like a loosening around the experience. Here is an example.

Lots of chatter of women outside the hall makes me start thinking I should do something: close the door tighter, get up to say something to them. Recognize my immediate knee jerk to "do something." Just sit and recognize gratefulness and happiness that I am sitting and not part of their conversation. Anger arises—mostly the feeling, not so much thoughts. I hold it like a baby. Women's voices are becoming tedious and seem to parallel my experience of the tediousness of self-creation. Wonder if it is possible to truly empty of self? . . . Sounds of women's voices seem to pass through my ears as if there is a channel through my head. It is a very open definite channel. I am not holding the sounds.

In this sitting, the meditator allowed her feelings of anger at being disturbed by women talking. There was a certain amount of building on the feelings, enough to make her want to get up and do something about it. She restrained herself from doing anything but still let herself feel the anger. She held the emotion "like a baby" and went on to contemplate how the women's voices were similar to her own self-created dialogues that ran through her sittings. Eventually she found herself in a state of mind where she was not holding the sounds. She was still experiencing the women's voices but was not taking them up as something she had to take care of, as she had earlier on in the sitting. They were just sounds entering her ears and nothing more.

Though in this case the end result was that her irritation at the women's voices vanished, that doesn't necessarily have to be the case with the non–taking-up process. With certain emotions that tend to linger and have an effect on our body chemistry, we may experience the feeling persist while we are no longer taking up any kind of building upon or elaboration of the experience. This is most noticeable with anxiety or fear. You could get to the point of no longer being afraid or anxious and yet still feel those sensations. In meditation practices where such emotions are equated with corresponding physical sensations, the meditator often believes that the sensations must cease in order for her or him to become free of the emotion. Instead, the emotion can cease but leave residual sensations. That is, you can still have a bodily experience of being anxious even while your mind is calm. This is a subtle, however easily discernible, indication that the non–taking-up process is the dominant process.

In this kind of situation it may still be hard to discern whether you're in a receptive process or a non–taking-up one. In a receptive process, you're drawn into and build upon the mental scenarios, thoughts, and feelings, while in a non–taking-up process, they tend to pass by without your being pulled into them—or the mental scenarios simply don't arise at all.

Not Believing in Self

In the previous example, the meditator mentions that she "wondered if it is possible to truly empty of self." Most Buddhist meditators believe that it is possible, even though it's not so easy to accomplish. Many Buddhist meditation practices approach this directly by giving instructions and teachings on seeing your experience in terms of no-self. And you can enter the non–taking-up process through those means, but because they are often directed, they generally employ a generative process to get there.

In going through a process of unlearning meditation we are not trying to employ some concept, image, or practice of no-self in order to see that there is no self. Instead, we are having experiences of self and seeing into them in such a way that the nonself, or dependently arisen nature, of them is known. For the purpose of talking about this, I tend to use the compound word *self-structure* for what we normally call self. What we are seeing is *not* a self but a way of perceiving and structuring our experiences as having a self. This way of structuring our experience as belonging to us, identifying us, and defining us gets seen in our explorations and contemplations within our meditation sittings. But this happens only because we have let ourselves own and identify with those experiences during the meditation sitting and because we have recollected aspects of that afterward.

This whole phenomenon of building a self-structure out of our experiences has great depth and subtlety to it. It exists in our projections onto others and the kind of transference we have with them. This area is outside the scope of this book, but I would like to touch on it briefly as it applies to how we take things up and to the non–taking-up process. To aid in this exploration, I will introduce a simpler concept than the psychodynamic mentioned above. This is a concept of "imaginary relationships with real people."

All of our relationships, even the one we have with ourself, are in some ways imaginary. In meditation we will have many rehearsed or imaginary dialogues with people, and we may come to certain conclusions about them and us from participating in those thoughts. We may see how our decision of seeing somebody as right or wrong, good or bad, friendly or hostile, affects how we feel about the person and informs our actions toward him or her. By defining someone else as a self with substantial and enduring qualities in our inner dialogues, we may inadvertently be sustaining a particular self-structure for ourselves. Usually these kinds of self-structure are difficult, if not impossible, to notice—when we are in them, we are them.

What can begin to happen in meditation is that by allowing *your mind as it is* into your meditation sittings, you will be taking up one self-structure after another through the course of being with your thoughts and feelings. When you are angry, it may not always be just a simple sensation that you identify as anger. That feeling of anger and the energy to act on it, when sat with and tolerated, may begin to reveal that it is held together somehow. It is not loose and flowing but tight and sticky. It is like the instances when you were angry at someone about something. Even without the memory of those particular instances, you may feel a familiar identity in the anger. The way you see the other person may also be familiar. He or she may appear threatening, belittling, or cold, and may exhibit any number of upsetting or irritating qualities.

It may take many rounds of going through emotionally difficult and painful sittings to develop this kind of awareness of self-structures. Even when we know better, we keep taking up these old, and for some reason trusted, selves, and we feed them the nourishment they seek. This is not something you can just transcend and be done with, though I wish it were so. This is a state of affairs that we need to learn how to disentangle ourselves from.

The non–taking-up of self-structures is just this type of disentangling. It may not be total or complete when it happens, as this is a process and not a fixed state, but it allows us not to take up a self we once were. This is different from the experience of not taking up the sensation of anger when it arises and passes away quickly. It is the experience of *not* taking up the angry person you feel yourself becoming at that time.

22

The Connected Process

The connected process generally occurs in the *samadhi* or *jhana* states mentioned in an earlier chapter but not in the pre-*jhanic* or hypnagogic states, which is one way to tell those states apart. It is the most "meditative" of all the six processes, as it fits the main definition of what traditional meditation is supposed to be: a unified state of mind. It is the meditative process where your attention is connected with an object of awareness, like the breath, a sound, or a visual image. That is why I call it a connected process instead of a unifying process, though that would be an equally accurate way of designating this particular meditative process.

Experiences of a connected or unifying nature have some common features. They often come with a loss of ordinary self-preoccupations and personality. For many people they seem to engender an experience of a transcendent or higher self (a pure consciousness). There can be a knowledge or intuition of a metaphysical reality that is beyond the mundane mind within these experiences. You may feel not only that such experiences connect you with a higher truth but also that the experiences themselves are the higher truth, to the extent that you're inclined to define such a truth as being synonymous with the experience of it.

On the surface, the connected process doesn't seem like a process, since it is not experienced as changing. It seems too stable, fixed and solid to fit in with our ordinary notions of a mind that is continuously in flux. By its very stability, it is like a mountain that rests under a veil of clouds, in that when it is discovered, it seems as though it has always been there. Thus there is often a perception of eternity with certain connected experiences. It replaces the self as the ground of your subjective reality while it is present. When it vanishes and you return to more ordinary modes of consciousness, you can easily believe that it always exists, for that is a part of the connected process (the belief in an eternal, stable reality somewhere). Here are a couple of instances of how the views inherent in the connected process come up when someone is in a *samadhi* state, taken from a journal by a student who has been working closely with me for the past five years.

I immediately enter into *samadhi*. As meditation continues I wonder if I am actually in *samadhi* throughout meditation. Different view—that the *samadhi* is always there to some extent—what changes is whether I am perceiving it.

And in another sitting around the same time, the student writes:

I pick up that I have some more-subtle attachment to this satisfied state of mind I have been in—that is, some subtle belief that it will last or that it is who I am.

Arriving at prescribed connected experiences is the goal of many meditation practices. Generally, the means to that goal is through generative practices, such as focusing on an image, concentrating on a mantra, or watching the breath. One seldom reads or hears of someone arriving at unifying (or transcendent) experiences through a receptive process. The common notion then is that such a powerful and complete loss of the separateness of an ordinary self can only come about through great feats of concentration and applied effort.

But the connected process, and the experiences that go with it, are sometimes described in terms of surrender. You surrender your attachments, your ego, or you just let go and merge with a divine essence. These are typical descriptions of following a generative practice, such as concentrating on a single-syllable mantra and then letting go of that practice once it has gotten you to a place of peace and concentration. Then the receptive process takes over for a little while until the mind finds that which it can connect with so thoroughly as to lose its sense of separateness.

Theravadin Buddhists, along with some other schools of Buddhism, see the connected process as having two distinct forms: those with wisdom and those without wisdom. The perception of not having wisdom in unified states of mind is when you have beliefs about the transcendent, eternal, unchanging nature of those unified states, but in other traditions, such as Vedanta, these beliefs would be seen as knowledge. This is one major area where Theravada and some other schools of Buddhism disagree with Hindu and other theistic teachings. My position on this in regard to unlearning meditation is that if you have connected experiences and believe in the transcendent, unchanging nature of them, then you can loosen your hold on those beliefs and begin to examine them, just as you've done with the meditation instructions. Those beliefs may carry a truth for you, which you can look into and verify or disprove for yourself over time.

The connected experiences with wisdom, from the Theravadin perspective, are those that are seen as changing mental constructs. They appear to be of a higher self or of a merging with a transcendent reality or essence, but when looked at closely, they are just as much mental constructs as our mundane, worldly experiences of mind. The wisdom lies in seeing mental constructs in connected states for what they are: products of the mind, not external or transcendent realities.

The connected process comprises only those *samadhi* states that are focusing and absorbing. It does not include those that are drifting, internally fluid, apparently empty, or rapidly changing. Such *samadhi* states may actually arise more within a receptive, explorative, or more particularly, a non–taking-up process. In this respect, the connected and non–taking-up processes are opposites, much like the generative and receptive processes are.

23

How to Use these Meditative
Processes Skillfully

It is best to use this model of six meditative processes to reflect on segments of a sitting after it's over. Often when people try to apply the processes during the sitting, they turn them into a labeling technique. Someone might just call off to himself that he is receptive, then conflicted, and so on, without gaining much insight into what is going on in his experience. Sometimes people will do this as a way to learn how to identify these processes, but I suggest you learn about these processes after the sitting, from having read your honest descriptions of your experiences in your own words from your journal.

Along these lines, I would suggest that you don't overuse these six processes in your descriptions of experiences, whether in a journal or in a dialogue with a teacher. Doing so could easily turn them into jargon, which would inhibit their usefulness as tools for exploring your experiences more deeply and learning about the interaction between the conditions that create your experiences and the ways you relate to them.

These six processes are concepts about experiences and so should not be granted some kind of exalted status of being the "truth" about our meditative experience. There are no definitive experiences of any of the meditative processes—no single experience can describe a process. There is no one experience of non–taking up, for example, though in some traditions it is taught that there is.

In practice, the six meditative processes actually become less separable as time goes on, less clearly delineated as we keep learning about them. They are helpful in the beginning to make discernments between different practices and to help us make choices about which practices meet with the conditions of our experiences. So you might be able to see how each process is different and separate, but after a while, they begin to overlap more and more and can be seen to be interrelated. This is because in unlearning meditation, all of the six meditative processes are known and cultivated equally, even the conflicted and generative.

Meditation Practices and Their Goals

Below is a table listing different meditation practices. To the right of each entry is the type of instruction one is taught to do when beginning that practice. To the right of that is the kind of meditative process that I assume is the goal or objective of that particular practice.

Name of Practice	Type of Practice	Goal Process
Metta—loving-kindness	Generative	Connected
Concentrated on the breath	Generative	Connected
Noting "in" and "out" with each breath	Generative	Non–taking up or connected
Noticing the natural breath	Receptive	Non–taking up or connected
Mantra meditation	Generative	Connected
Body scanning	Generative	Non–taking up
Guided meditation	Generative	Connected or non–taking up
Choiceless awareness	Generative or receptive	Non–taking up
Just sitting (Shikantaza)	Receptive	Non–taking up

Jhana practice	Generative	Connected
Noting (Mahasi method)	Generative	Non–taking up
Recollective Awareness (unlearning meditation)	Receptive	Conflicted, generative, explorative, non–taking up, and connected

This table illustrates how meditation practices can begin with instructions based on one type of meditation practice and yet lead to a different meditative process. Often, however, the meditative practice is presented to students highlighting the developed process it can lead to (its goal) instead of the basic process it incorporates in the instructions. For example, when you practice meditating with a single-syllable mantra, the method of doing the practice is to repeat the mantra over and over. The goal of the practice, however, is to become completely absorbed and concentrated on the mantra and enter into a state of unified consciousness. If that form of meditation were presented without such a goal, then the stated objective would be the constant repetition of the mantra in and of itself.

Even though each of the meditation practices listed in the table can lead to processes or meditative experiences different from the one(s) stated, they are often taught as though they lead to only one process. Other processes that arise while doing those practices are not usually considered acceptable and are thus either devalued or dismissed. It is quite possible, and even likely, that someone practicing awareness of the breath will not arrive at a connected or non–taking-up process for some time. The person doing that practice would more quickly find himself in a conflicted process, in periods of struggle around the instructions, or in a receptive process, giving up doing the instructions altogether for a while. Both of these processes would be considered "outside" of the breath-awareness practice. Yet they are occurring within the practice. This is the case with each meditation practice you are taught: meditative processes you experience that are not part of the goal of the practice are excluded from that practice rather than included in it.

In the case of Recollective Awareness Meditation, however, all six meditative processes have a role and function within the practice. The nature of the practice is receptive, but it can lead into the other five processes, including them in significant ways. That is one reason why I do not state a goal for this type of meditation. If I did, it would eclipse and exclude the naturally arising processes that come from sitting in a receptive manner. Instead, by including everything experienced in meditation, there is no single experience that is its goal. Where meditation leads is a result of how you engage, develop, and learn from these six meditative processes in a lifelong path.

PART FOUR

Leveling
the Hierarchy
of Experiences

24

Assessing Meditative States

It is quite natural for us to develop a hierarchy of meditative states. At the top are what we consider optimal states of mind, such as mental clarity, equanimity, mindfulness, and deeply tranquil experiences that are wakeful. Near the bottom are those experiences that are considered mundane or uninteresting. Generally, at the very bottom are negative emotional or painful states of mind.

This hierarchy of meditative states may not be explicitly stated in anything you have read or heard, but it has been reinforced by other meditators and teachers alike. It comes up as a word or phrase describing how you feel about an experience. Or it is seen right there in the meditation sitting as part of the running commentary on your experiences.

When I ask people to look at how this hierarchy operates in their sittings, they sometimes feel as though they are being asked to let go of the optimal states they experience. That is not the case. It is not about letting go of optimal states but about seeing into how you assess your experiences using them as the standard for comparison. And by asking you to look at those experiences that have been devalued on account of such comparisons, I am not asking you to dwell on those experiences but to consider that by devaluing them it becomes hard for you to be with them and learn from them.

As you continue to meditate, you may find that many experiences have not been assessed within your existing hierarchy. That is primarily because they have gone by largely unnoticed. For usually as our experience gets subtler and subtler, it also gets harder to put into existing language, which consequently makes it harder to identify and thus harder to evaluate. You can't really evaluate something that you are dimly aware of, except maybe to say that it is "strange, mysterious, or indefinable." By putting language to these experiences, we also fit them into our hierarchy.

You may think that assessing and evaluating experiences in meditation that have not undergone this process is moving in the wrong direction. Shouldn't we be going in the direction of having no preferences? That's a noble goal but highly unrealistic, and in practice, it tends to lead to a lack of discernment. Discerning wisdom not only knows the differences between qualities of mind but also knows their value in terms of the path toward awakening.

For instance, by noticing a subtle quality of compassion in an internal dialogue that in the past you would have ignored as mundane thinking, that experience can become valued. Then, instead of becoming concerned at having been engrossed in a fanciful inner dialogue, you become able to see that there was real thoughtfulness and caring for the individual in your thoughts. The experience then naturally moves to another place in your inner hierarchy of mind states.

States of mind that are labeled as negative may arise at times when good qualities are also present. If you label the state of mind as negative when some compassion or understanding is also present, you will put an experience that is wholesome and beneficial in a place in which it is to be "overcome" instead of developed. Wouldn't you want to develop more compassion for yourself when you are upset at somebody? When compassion does arise within an internal dialogue, or actual situation, of being upset, wouldn't that compassion be something you would then want to cultivate? Should such beneficial states of mind be seen with an all-or-nothing view, where it has to be absolute compassion with no trace of ill will? With such an absolute view, many wholesome and beneficial states that arise in the course of meditation may be erroneously evaluated as worthless or a waste of time.

Part of the problem here lies in assessing an experience on the basis of a single prominent characteristic. This often happens when we conclude what an experience is before having investigated it thoroughly. When we explore our experiences, it is likely that the judgment we have of them will also change because we become aware of more of what is going on. So during a patch of anger in a meditation sitting, you might also notice hurt, fear, and periods of being less invested in it and more gentle. Acknowledging the gentleness might be a way to see the experience as not wholly negative but also containing a positive element. By acknowledging that, the experience can shift from being at the bottom of the hierarchy to somewhere closer to the middle, where it becomes easier to accept. It is still not perfect, not at the top, but it is no longer in the rubbish bin.

State-Dependent Qualities

The notion of qualities, abilities, and inner resources being dependent on one's state of mind is a familiar one in psychology but is not used that often in meditation teaching. Yet it is found in the discourses of the Buddha. The basic theory is that the state of mind we are in greatly affects the qualities that can be accessed. For example, when we are in a deeply calm state, especially one of the pre-*jhanic* states, we may be able to notice what is occurring while in it, but when we come out and return to a more normal waking state, we have no memory of what went on. Awareness does not seem to bridge the two states. The quality of awareness in the calm state is not the same as the quality of awareness in a normal waking state. These two separate states of consciousness have a different kind of awareness. They may also have different kinds of concentration, effort, and ways of feeling and thinking.

When you look at the concept of consciousness from a Buddhist perspective, it is not an entity such as a self, but a way of knowing your experience. Changes in states of consciousness are thus changes in ways of knowing. When we go from one state of consciousness to another, we not only feel differently, we perceive things differently. This is how we experience the difference between deep sleep, . waking, pre-*jhanic* states, and chemically induced altered states. They seem like completely different worlds, with one not so easily relating to, or intersecting with, any of the others.

So it should be no surprise that certain qualities of mind that you develop in meditation will appear to be different and function differently in other states of consciousness. Otherwise we then tend to make the assumption that a quality is entirely absent in a state, when it may just be manifesting in that state in a different way. Awareness as it functions in hypnagogic or pre-*jhanic* states and in waking states is an example of this—we may tend to think that awareness is absent in our pre-*jhanic* states because we can't remember anything when we come out of them, when, in truth, during those states there are periods of being aware.

By not seeing and acknowledging the qualities in certain states of mind, we may devalue those experiences. Sometimes we are so busy looking for certain qualities to be present, as when we look for some kind of clear, sharp awareness in our calm states, thus missing what qualities are more easily observed, such as the peace or stillness of mind that could be found in them. We might also have the idea that we should be able to do things in certain states of mind, such as focus on a meditation object for a long period of time, when that may not be possible. Looking at qualities and abilities as being state dependent helps us get a realistic picture of what is actually possible in the states of consciousness we go through inside and out of meditation.

Optimal States of Mind

Optimal states of mind are often believed to be the goal of meditation. When we arrive at an optimal state of mind in our meditation sittings, we usually recognize it as such. We know we would like to have this state of mind last longer. It often becomes a standard to measure other, less-optimal experiences and states of consciousness. If it has not immediately changed our view of the nature of reality or the truth of existence, it most likely will as we hold on to it, remember it, and try to reenter it or re-create it. Our tendency is to take an optimal state of mind to be a realization or an experience of a truth when it agrees with the descriptions we've heard.

What interests me about this in the context of unlearning meditation is how these optimal states function for us. They can work for us at times, against us at other times. They work for us by giving us confidence in ourselves as meditators and trust in the meditative process, as well as in our teachers and their particular teachings and traditions. They do this by bringing the teachings closer to our experience—instead of trying to experience the states of mind we hear about, we now have our own experience of those states of mind. It is no longer someone else's experience that we reference when we hear people speak of such meditative states but our very own.

On the downside, however, we can develop a certain amount of pride, ownership, and self-identification around such experiences, for now that they are our own, we can make something out of ourselves on account of them. This can be a very subtle thing. It may not be much of an impediment for some people, while for others, it may infect their minds to the degree that they cannot settle for anything less. For them, optimal states become something they need to experience in each meditation sitting, and so when they go through periods of not having such experiences, they either must live off the memories of past optimal states or feel deprived of them. Such deprivation can be awfully deflating and even lead to giving up meditation practice altogether.

It is here that unlearning your reliance on optimal experiences in meditation may become necessary. You can see things about yourself and learn from all of your experiences, not only the optimal ones. You may need to remind yourself at times that this has indeed been the case. Then you may find it easier to let go of the need to have an optimal state of mind in order to investigate your experience—though you might still prefer an optimal state to any other that comes along. That is perfectly natural, totally human. It is not about removing optimal states from the top of the hierarchy, or doubting their usefulness and skillfulness, but about not getting so attached to them that you disregard everything else.

Attainments

Attainments are an integral part of meditation practice, especially within more traditional settings. When learning Zen from a *roshi* or Vipassana from a Theravadin monk, for instance, you'll most likely hear about the kind of enlightenment or awakening experience that will happen to you if you follow that practice. Those experiences are often considered attainments, which are permanent and irreversible, and they can indicate a certain knowledge that can't be lost, certain negative qualities that have been shed, or a certain connection with a higher truth or ultimate reality.

Attainments are often granted by teachers after the student has reported an experience or realization that matches what the attainment is said to be in the teacher's tradition. A meditator will rarely claim an attainment for himself without verifying it with a teacher, since such attainments often carry with them the status of now being a part of the tradition in a significant way and often pave the way for the student's becoming a teacher within that tradition.

Many people who have been granted attainments trust in their teacher's assessment of their progress in meditation and consequently believe in the validity of their attainments. Others may question whether it is true or not. Early on in my own experience, when my teacher told me I was a *sotapanna,* a stream-enterer (the first of four stages culminating in final liberation), I believed him for about twenty-four hours, and then it stuck me, "How can he know?" So I took it upon myself to learn more about how he came to that assessment. I studied the texts used to chart a student's progress in meditation toward becoming a stream-enterer. I consulted other monks who were knowledgeable in this area, including my teacher at the time, to ascertain how they knew when someone had become a stream-enterer. And I talked with other monks who had also been told that they had that attainment. I also inquired into the experiences that they had told to their teachers when they were granted their attainment. From these conversations and my own study and reflections, which were done gradually over a two-year period, I came to a simple conclusion: teachers do not know their students well enough to make such claims for them.

This conclusion may be a bit shocking for you, especially if you have been told you have an attainment by a wise, selfless, compassionate, venerable teacher. How well does your teacher actually know you? Does he or she know you better than you know yourself? In these cases, students often do believe that the teacher has some special ability to see into their minds and know with certainty that they have arrived at a particular attainment. The Buddha was said to have this ability. But that does not mean that modern-day meditation teachers have it too.

All of this comes down to whether you can find the attainment verified within your own experience. To verify an attainment in your own experience takes time, learning, and honesty. The time factor lies in suspending belief in the certainty of the attainment and entertaining it as a possibility for a period of time. This opens the door for honesty around it. You are then able to look at aspects of yourself that may not have changed due to the attainment experience and consider whether the attainment has actually seeped into those areas. You can also notice those changes that have occurred on account of the attainment that agree with the teachings regarding that attainment and see confirmation in them. But you still don't have to decide either way as to whether you have the attainment or not, though it may at times feel distressing not to know for certain. Here is where additional learning can help. When studying the teachings regarding attainments in various traditions, you can get a better idea of what changes with an attainment as stated in the texts, as opposed to what is believed by your teachers and fellow practitioners in a particular tradition. In some cases, such as in Vipassana, the Pali canon has different descriptions than those that are found in the later commentarial texts that modern-day teachers generally consult. This discrepancy can open up a whole can of worms in regard to whether the modern versions are corrupt or, in the opposite direction, whether the earlier versions are incomplete or poorly stated.

There may be no way to prove an attainment beyond the shadow of a doubt, and all of this work to verify it may be one huge distraction from the practice of meditating. I have followed the approach of not talking about attainments with students, keeping my teaching free of this whole business. Instead, I prefer to talk about people's development in meditation in terms of discernible qualities being present with more frequency, having greater influence on their decisions and actions. The various qualities that together would be seen to make up a description of a particular attainment are part of this picture, but without all the stuff around being someone who has a certain attainment and therefore "possesses" these qualities.

When you take away the need to ascribe an attainment to someone in order to acknowledge a difference in how the person is, there is a freedom from creating a self around those qualities— there is no person who is identified as being such and such on account of what the teacher has told him or her. What there is is a humble person who is becoming aware and awake, and who manifests self-honesty, wisdom, patience, friendliness, compassion, and other excellent human qualities.

A Postscript to Unlearning Meditation

Unlearning meditation is an open-ended process, so much so, that after a while, you might find your meditation practice to be so open and free that it is hard to recall what it was like to meditate in a way that felt rigid, pressured, and result oriented. The doubts, anxieties, and concerns about a receptive approach to meditation tend to die down considerably over time, though they may not vanish altogether. When someone asks what you do when you meditate, you might find it hard to give a clear and precise answer. As you continue, the meditation practice becomes less defined, less tangible, and less conceptual. It becomes loose and diffuse.

Its emptiness becomes more and more apparent. Because you are seldom doing anything in meditation, your mind experiences stretches of being empty of doing. Because rarely is anything added to your experience, your meditations become empty of instructions, strategies, goals, and judgments. Because nothing is being subtracted from your experience, your meditations include all that would naturally be present in your mind, and as such, your mind becomes empty of avoidance and self-deception.

What captures your attention begins to hold your interest in a more sustained way. You can stay with it, even though it may hurt to do so, waiting patiently, not for it to go away, but for an exploration into the dependently arisen nature of the experience to begin. You may find that the quality of interest while meditating feels calm and steady, unlike something driven by desires, which is nourished by each new discovery on how things came to be in your life.

Your mind goes into so many different states of consciousness—from a full range of degrees of wakefulness to levels of *samadhi* and modes of sleep—that you can no longer believe that only one state of mind is optimal, true, or real. The whole of the human mind in all of its great variety is now your arena, and you can go from the heights to the depths and all that is in between with a sense of confidence that what you experience, see, and know are constructions of the mind and are no more true or real than that.

And when you wonder if there is some instruction you must do, some state of mind you should generate, or some truth you must realize, you can pause and look into those thoughts without having to believe them. You are not going to be turned away from your own path so easily again. You have developed greater trust and confidence in the meditative process, which is none other than trust in the path of inner awakening, otherwise known as the Dharma.

Acknowledgments

This book has had a long genesis, with many individuals participating in its development in a variety of ways. It started in 1998
after I showed Jeremy Tarcher (founder of Tarcher Press) some
of my writings on meditation, and he encouraged me to write a
book. The title "Unlearning Meditation" came out of the several
conversations we had. I wish to thank him for his support and
counsel in the creation of the first version of the manuscript and
for his believing in the value of this book.

The original 1999 version of *Unlearning Meditation* was dedicated to a dear friend, student, and colleague, Gordon Smith, who
passed away in 2006. Gordon helped me establish the Skillful
Meditation Project, served as the treasurer, and provided financial
support for the organization at critical times. Many of my students
from the early 1990s fondly remember Sunday afternoon sittings
at Gordon's house in the hills of Mount Washington, situated between downtown Los Angeles and Pasadena.

My wife, Jacquelin, who has been in my life since before I
left for Nepal (she followed three months later), helped behind
the scenes with the writing of this book, and she read it in her

accustomed thorough manner. Her observations and suggestions have clarified many passages that otherwise might have been misinterpreted.

Dave O'Neal, senior editor at Shambhala Publications, brought my work to the attention of Shambhala Publications and has shepherded it from the initial proposal to the final draft. His care and understanding are evident throughout the book.

Over the past decade I have been training people to teach Recollective Awareness Meditation. The first person I trained as a teacher is Ron Sharrin, who is a psychotherapist and longtime Buddhist meditator living in Topanga Canyon, California. He attended one of my retreats in 1996 and I began teaching him how to teach this approach to meditation in 1999. Mary Webster, who lives in Spokane, Washington, followed a couple of years later, and she is unique in that I was her first meditation teacher almost fifteen years ago. Another longtime student, Linda Modaro, has been studying meditation with me for the past decade and primarily teaches in Santa Monica. Nelly Kaufer has been teaching meditation for nearly twenty years in the Portland area and for the last five years has been working with students in this approach. Dan Nussbaum is a teacher who leads groups in Los Angeles. Greg Bantick, who has a long history of meditation practice, is another teacher I have trained. We met on my first trip to Australia in 2004 and he now teaches this approach to groups in Brisbane and Northern New South Wales.

There are several meditation teachers in Australia who have more or less adopted this approach to meditation, though some of them may blend it with other forms of meditation. I would like to mention Winton Higgins in Sydney, Victor von der Heyde in Sydney and Brisbane, Anna Markey in Adelaide, Jenny Taylor in Alice Springs, Eoin Meades in Brisbane, John and Bobbi Allan in Lismore, Ken Golding, Barry Farrin, Nique Murch, Marc Wilson, Betsy Faen and Malcolm Huxter. I would like to express special appreciation for my dear friend and traveling companion Eoin Meades. We visited Sri Lanka in 2005 and Tibet and Nepal two years later. Eoin has been encouraging me to write this book for several years. There are many folks in Australia I would wish to thank for their kindness and generosity. One person in particular, who has been my host in Sydney, is Paul Frischknecht.

Many of my students over the years have assisted in a variety of ways in the preparation of this book. I would like to thank Larry Heliker, Len Follick, Deborah Wozniak, Baljinder Sahdra, Sue Lucksted, Anna Delacroix, Brian Bush, Adrienne House, David Clark, Brad Crampton, Tatiana Melnyk, and Paul Freedman. Others who have helped me include Grady McGonagill, Sarah Conover, Cynthia Schroeder, and Karen Hastings. Also, I would like to acknowledge Peter Mackie of Sydney, Australia, for allowing me to use his creative journal entries. There are also many other students whose presence has contributed to the thought and writing of this book. I offer them my gratitude.

I would like to thank Mu Soeng and Andrew Olendzki, the co-directors of the Barre Center for Buddhist Studies, where I teach a weekend retreat every year. Over the last couple of years I have also led retreats at Cloud Mountain Retreat Center in Washington state, and would like to thank Dhammadasa for inviting me to teach there. Various Vipassana communities have also invited me teach workshops and retreats over the years. I wish to thank the Spokane Vipassana Meditation Community, Santa Fe Vipassana Sangha, the Albuquerque Vipassana Sangha, the White Heron Sangha, and the Bluegum Sangha.

I tend to refine my ideas in four distinct ways. One is through my own contemplation. The second is by writing down my thoughts. The third is by giving talks on retreats. The fourth is through in-depth conversations with colleagues. Most of my colleagues are teachers I have trained, but there are others who are Dharma teachers, educators, and writers I have had the good fortune to spend some concentrated time with. The late Nyanaponika Mahathera, author of *The Heart of Buddhist Meditation,* greatly influenced my subsequent reflections on the Mahasi method during the two conversations we had when I was a monk in Sri Lanka. When I came back to the States in 1990, I was fortunate to have Dharma conversations with the late Ratanasara Mahathera, and later with the eminent Sri Lankan Buddhist scholar, Dr. Ananda Guruge. I would like to express my gratitude to Stephen Batchelor, Ken McLeod, William Waldron, Tony Duff, and Joseph Goldstein for the engaging discussions we have had over the past few years. The person I regularly exchange ideas with is my dear Idyllwild friend Sam Crowell.

The generous support of my students over the years has provided me with enough financial security to take the time to write. Their donations to the Skillful Meditation Project have made this book truly possible. I wish to give special thanks to the late Gordon Smith (and his brother Greg), Mary Renard, Nancy Holt, and Wayne Chavez.

Lastly, I would like to express appreciation for my teachers, mentors, and friends during the period of my nine years in South Asia, and the first few years of my return to the United States. First, I would like to mention the teachers at the Campus of International Languages in Kathmandu from 1982 to 1986, the monks at Kanduboda Meditation Center in Sri Lanka from 1987 to 1988, the monks at the Island Hermitage from 1988 to 1990, and the late Godwin Samararatne at the Nilambe Meditation Center, where I taught meditation for six months in 1989. I would like to mention the teachers, students, and staff at Ryokan College from 1991 to 1992, and my supervisors and fellow psychotherapy interns at the Saturday Center for Psychotherapy from 1992 to 1994, all of whom were a great help to me upon my return to Los Angeles. From that period in my life I would also like to acknowledge Dr. Jock Hearn, a Zen monk and psychotherapist, who showed me the possibilities for a young Buddhist ex-monk teaching the Dharma in the West.

Jason Siff
Idyllwild, California
November 2009

INDEX

Page numbers in *italic* type refer to words found in the meditation journal entries used in this book.

instruction-centered practices, 14, 110

instructions. *See* meditation instructions; meditation practices; Recollective Awareness Meditation

intentions, 11–14, 21, 27–28, 35, 37, 66–67, 137–38, 148, 159, 170

interest, x–xi, 52, *64–66*, 74, 122, 128, 160, *168–69*, 195, 199

internal dialogues, 50, 161, *162*, 177, 192
   rehashing conversations, 35, 42, 52, *77*
   rehearsing, 42, 179
   with your meditation teacher, 50

interpretation, 6, 32, 44, 80, 127, 164, 171

investigation, 63–66, 84, 95. *See also* exploration

jhana, 123–126, 131–33, 181, 187. See also *samadhi*

journaling, 15–19, 50, 53–55, 185
   instructions for, 17–19,

joy, 4, 29, 60, 65, 124, 128

judging, 15, 26, 52, 76, *77–78*, *88–89*, 107, 139, 193

karma, 167–68

knowledge, 29, 42–44, 64, 93, 181, 183, 196

labels, 53, 65–66, 97, 106, 171, 175, 192

language, 39–44, 53, 97, 115, 120, 133

laziness, 124

learning, 41, 47, 60, 63, 74, 147–48, 158, 185–86, 197

letting go, 106, 126, 159, 177, 183

liberation, final, 132–33, 196

loneliness, 32, *81–82*, 103

lucid dreaming, 125

lust, *60*, *153*

Mahasi method, 7–8, 32, 57, 175, 187, 203

Mahathera Narada, 40

Manjusri, *162*

mantra meditation, 4–5, 48, 72, 105, 111, 126, 182, 186

McLeod, Ken, 158

meditation
   assumptions about, 139, 142
   common perception of, 14, 72, 109–110, 141, 182
   goal of, 34, 144, 175–76, 182, 186–87, 194, 199
   guided, 105–6, 144, 158
   promise of, 3, 12, 33–34

meditation instructions, 3, 12–13, 138–39
   contradictions in, 23, 176
   loosening around, 12, 93–94, 183

meditation practices
   traditional, xi, 3, 14–15, 39, 57, 141, 158, 181, 196–98
   Eastern, 47–48

meditative process, the, 139, 145, 195, 200
   theory of, 140–48, 161–84, 186–87

meditative states, hierarchy of, 191–94, 196

meditators, beginning, 4, 27–30

memories, 15–16, 25–26, 37, 61, 80–81, *81*, 99, 128, 144, *153*, 154, 168
   painful, 36, 145, 163

pleasant, 195
repetitive, 73
mental constructs, 95, 183
building, 139, 173, 176–79
models, 47, 96, 101, 140, 170, 185
mental images, visual, 4, 115, *116*, 118, 125–29, *130*, *152*, *154*, *169*, 181
colors, *111*, *115*, 122, 126–27, 166
lights, 44, 94, 122, 124, *126–27*, 129, *163*
moving, *90*, *117*, *128–29*
random, 127–28, 130, *151–53*
metaphors, 40–41, 84
metta (loving-kindness), 143, 150, 164, 167–68, 186
mindfulness, 15, 57–58, 85, 169, 172, 191. *See also* awareness; Mahasi method
mind-wandering, 4, 13, 22, 86–87, 149, *152–53*
monkey mind, 39, 42
monks, 7, 197, 203–4
morals, 132, 146
multilinearity, 118

naming, 32, 96–97, 99, 101–3, 171
narratives, 49–50, 52, 100–101, 103
personal, 47–49, *81*, 95, 99–100
Nepal, 5
non–taking-up, 155, 161, 173–74, 176, 178, 180, 186–87
non–taking-up process, 140, 173–79, 184
nonself, 178
no-self, 26, 48, 103, 178

objects
concentration, 126, 149–50, 181

mental, 43, 86, 175
primary, 14, 32, 108–110, 150, 157–58, 176
sense, 43, 125, 175
Om, *159*
Oneness. *See* unifying experiences; transcendance
optimal states, 176, 191, 194–96
out-of-body experiences, 125

Pali language, 41
path, 47, 96, 100, 132–33, 146, 148, 192, 200
patience, 9, 51, 59, *60*, 61, 67, 72–73, 94, 198
peace, 18, 33, 60, 102–3, 124, 128, 183, 194
perception, 40, 65, 124
planning, 14, 39, 42–44, *60*, *66*, *115*
pleasure
meditative, 120–22, 125, 132–33
sensual, *115*
posture, 21, 22, 109
lotus, 5, 7
sitting, 14, 16
predicaments, 72–73, 79, 84–85, 90
problem solving, 14, 42,
psychology, xi, 6, 47, 51, 193

qualities, 57–67, 193–94

realization, 24, 48, 72, 87, 166, 195–96
receptive process, 140–42, 145, 151, 155, 157–60, 162, 178, 182–84, 187
receptivity, 142
recollecting, 15, 44, 49, 53–54, 65, *168–70*
effects of, 116–17, 120